THE PSYCHOLOGY OF CLIMATE CHANGE

What explains our attitudes towards the environment? Why do so many climate change initiatives fail? How can we do more to prevent humans damaging the environment?

The Psychology of Climate Change explores the evidence for our changing environment, and suggests that there are significant cognitive biases in how we think about, and act on climate change. The authors examine how organisations have attempted to mobilise the public in the fight against climate change, but these initiatives have often failed due to the public's unwillingness to adapt their behaviour. The authors also explore why some people deny climate change altogether, and the influence that these climate change deniers can have on global action to mitigate further damage.

By analysing our attitudes to the environment, *The Psychology of Climate Change* argues that we must think differently about climate change to protect our planet, as a matter of great urgency.

Geoffrey Beattie is Professor of Psychology at Edge Hill University. He is the author of more than 20 books and regularly appears in the media. In 2018, he was elected a Fellow of the Royal Society of Arts for his contribution to social change research.

Laura McGuire is a Postdoctoral Research Assistant at Edge Hill University. She explores possible psychological barriers which prevent people from living a more sustainable lifestyle.

THE PSYCHOLOGY OF EVERYTHING

The Psychology of Everything is a series of books which debunk the myths and pseudo-science surrounding some of life's biggest questions.

The series explores the hidden psychological factors that drive us, from our sub-conscious desires and aversions, to the innate social instincts handed to us across the generations. Accessible, informative, and always intriguing, each book is written by an expert in the field, examining how research-based knowledge compares with popular wisdom, and illustrating the potential of psychology to enrich our understanding of humanity and modern life.

Applying a psychological lens to an array of topics and contemporary concerns – from sex to addiction to conspiracy theories – The Psychology of Everything will make you look at everything in a new way.

Titles in the series:

The Psychology of Grief
Richard Gross

The Psychology of Sex
Meg-John Barker

The Psychology of Dieting
Jane Ogden

The Psychology of Performance
Stewart T. Cotterill

The Psychology of Trust
Ken J. Rotenberg

The Psychology of Working Life
Toon Taris

The Psychology of Conspiracy Theories
Jan-Willem van Prooijen

The Psychology of Addiction
Jenny Svanberg

The Psychology of Fashion
Carolyn Mair

The Psychology of Gardening
Harriet Gross

The Psychology of Gender
Gary W. Wood

The Psychology of Climate Change
Geoffrey Beattie

For further information about this series please visit
www.thepsychologyofeverything.co.uk.

THE PSYCHOLOGY
OF CLIMATE
CHANGE

GEOFFREY BEATTIE AND LAURA MCGUIRE

Routledge
Taylor & Francis Group

LONDON AND NEW YORK

First published 2019
by Routledge
2 Park Square, Milton Park, Abingdon, Oxon OX14 4RN

and by Routledge
711 Third Avenue, New York, NY 10017

Routledge is an imprint of the Taylor & Francis Group, an informa business

British Library Cataloguing-in-Publication Data
A catalogue record for this book is available from the British Library

Library of Congress Cataloging-in-Publication Data
A catalog record for this book has been requested

ISBN: 978-1-138-48451-1 (hbk)
ISBN: 978-1-138-48452-8 (pbk)
ISBN: 978-1-351-05182-8 (ebk)

Typeset in Joanna
by Apex CoVantage, LLC
Printed and bound by CPI Group (UK) Ltd, Croydon CR0 4YY

Visit https://www.routledge.com/The-Psychology-of-Everything/
book-series/POE

We would like to express our sincerest gratitude to John Cater, the Vice-Chancellor of Edge Hill University, and George Talbot, the Pro Vice-Chancellor for Research at the University, for their support and encouragement. Our research has been supported in recent years by the British Academy and by an Edge Hill University Graduate Teaching Assistant Award to Laura McGuire which allowed her to conduct her PhD in this area.

CONTENTS

1

INTRODUCTION

THE MAN ON THE BUS AND THE SCIENCE OF CLIMATE CHANGE

A BUS JOURNEY IN THE SNOW

Conversations with strangers on buses are often rather difficult. We all know that. It was probably the open notebook that attracted his attention. He kept glancing over at it, surreptitiously at first, and then with longer glances as if he wanted to be seen. The pure white page of the notebook had just two words on it. 'CLIMATE CHANGE!' in big bold pencil. He tutted on his third glance at the page and then started to speak abruptly. 'Well, that's bloody nonsense for a start,' he said. He pointed to the snow on the street. It was only a fine dusting, but it was enough. 'So that's global warming for you,' he said and looked at one of the authors to join him in some communal condemnation of this great hoax. He said it again, louder this time, and glanced around for support. He was starting to attract an audience; a number of our neighbours on the bus were nodding along to his comments, but he then turned back to the one nearest to him, the one crammed into the seat beside him, the one who couldn't move.

Perhaps he had been encouraged by the exclamation mark; perhaps that's what was responsible for the conversation in the first place. 'What a joke,' he continued. 'You don't believe in that rubbish, do you?' His look was accusatory, it demanded an answer. But what was the point in replying?

It seems that climate change, like politics, religion and death, has entered the domain of topics that are not discussed in polite conversation. There is just too much disagreement (not violent disagreement, of course, at least not yet, but still very heated and messy) linked to personal values, different ideologies, even religious views that cannot be bridged by polite words (although we will try in this book). It wouldn't have felt right talking about the difference between the weather and the climate to that man on the bus, or even trying to empathise with the fact that 'global warming' can be a highly misleading term for many. Some have suggested 'climate chaos' as a better descriptor of what is happening and what will happen more and more in the future. The concept of 'chaos' captures what we are witnessing in terms of more frequent, extreme and unpredictable weather patterns.

But it was probably not the best time for a lecture on climate chaos, nor was it the best time to point out that there is a *remarkable* scientific consensus on climate change – 'remarkable' because it is rare to see this degree of scientific agreement on anything. Science is, after all, fuelled by dispute, disagreement and difference. That indeed is its nature – that's how it develops and grows and *changes*. But when it comes to climate change, the scientists *agree* that there's been an increase in greenhouse gas concentrations in the atmosphere and that this is linked to a general warming of the planet. There is agreement that mean temperatures have increased over the past century and that they will continue to grow. They also agree that it is 'highly likely' that human beings have contributed to this through their behaviour, on the basis that these changes in greenhouse gas emissions and global warming have mirrored major changes in human activity, like the Industrial Revolution, and changing patterns of land use, energy demands and transport.

But the term 'highly likely' seems to be part of the problem. It's not 'certain,' the critics say, not like death itself (or taxes, as Benjamin Franklin wryly noted); it sounds woolly and vague to people unused to probabilistic reasoning. Climate scientists also agree that the impact of climate change on the planet will be severe, but with variability in exactly how severe. They have modelled a range of possible outcomes, but working out the exact probability of each possible outcome is more problematic because of degrees of uncertainty in the modelling, including knowledge of the earth's climate system and future human activity. That's the problem with science; it deals with probabilities and likelihoods.

WHAT THE SCIENTISTS SAY

The Intergovernmental Panel on Climate Change (IPCC), which comprises hundreds of the world's leading scientists, is the international agency charged with reviewing and evaluating the vast body of accumulating scientific evidence around climate change. It was awarded the Nobel Peace Prize in 2007. Over the past three decades, it has issued a succession of reports and 'consensus statements' summarising the current state of extant knowledge on climate change, with the accumulating evidence, still couched in probabilistic terms, pointing more and more to one inescapable conclusion.

In 1995, the IPCC concluded, 'The balance of evidence suggests a discernible human influence on the global climate.' In the 2007 report, the IPCC concluded,

> Human activities . . . are modifying the concentration of atmospheric constituents . . . that absorb or scatter radiant energy . . . Most of the observed warming over the last 50 years is very likely to have been due to the increase in greenhouse gas emissions.

In the 2013 report, the IPCC concluded, 'Warming of the climate system is *unequivocal* (italics added) and since the 1950s, many of the observed changes are unprecedented over decades to millennia . . . It is extremely likely that human influence has been the dominant cause.' In 2015, the IPCC concluded that they are 'now 95 percent certain that humans are the *main cause* of current global warming' (IPCC

2015: v; italics added). The IPCC also suggested that, on the basis of the existing evidence, a rise in global temperature will have 'severe and widespread impacts on . . . substantial species extinctions, large risks to global and regional food security . . . growing food or working outdoors,' as well as producing more extreme fluctuations in weather, including droughts, flooding and storms. The conclusions of the IPCC have been endorsed and supported by over 200 scientific agencies around the globe, including the principal scientific organisations in each of the G8 countries such as the National Academy of Science in the United States and the Royal Society in the United Kingdom.

Furthermore, an increasing number of people are witnessing the devastating effects of climate change first-hand, with increased adverse weather conditions such as frequent flooding, stronger hurricanes, longer heatwaves, more tsunamis and periods of drought (IPCC 2015; UK Climate Change Risk Assessment 2016). The World Health Organisation (WHO 2017) warns that with temperatures rising and the increase in rainfall, we need to be prepared for more illnesses resulting from climate change, including mosquito-borne infections such as malaria, dengue and the Zika virus. The WHO report, 'Climate change already claims tens of thousands of lives a year from diseases, heat and extreme weather,' and they say it is 'the greatest threat to global health in the 21st century.' Indeed, the World Economic Forum identified climate change as the top global risk facing humanity – a greater risk than weapons of mass destruction and severe water shortages (Global Risk Report 2016).

The evidence suggests that human beings are the most significant contributor to climate change through energy use, population growth, land use and patterns of consumption (IPCC 2015). Currently, CO_2 emissions from human activity are at their highest ever level and continue to rise. Global CO_2 emissions in 2011 were reported as being '150 times higher than they were in 1850' (World Resource Institute 2014, see also IPCC 2015). Although we cannot undo the damage already done with regards to climate change, we do have the power to adapt our behaviour to ameliorate any future effects.

Despite the fact that the role of human activity in its causation is 'clear' (and 'growing'), evidence for large-scale behavioural adaptation on the part of the public is absent. Indeed, there appears to be a monumental disconnect between the science of climate change, and the public's perception of climate change and their subsequent actions. For example, a 2013 survey by Yale University found that only 63% of Americans 'believe that global warming is happening.' Interestingly, this figure had been higher (72%) back in 2008, before the effects of the economic crisis were fully felt and before the 2009 'Climategate' scandal where emails of climate scientists at the University of East Anglia were hacked. It was suggested at the time that there had been some manipulation of the scientific data, and climate scientists, like everyone else in this great 'climate change debate,' had a vested interest to protect. Belief in climate change dropped to 52% in 2010. Nearly half of Americans in a 2010 survey thought that global warming was attributable to natural causes rather than being attributable to human activity – climate scientists clearly think otherwise.

The answer as to why there is such a great divide in opinions between scientists and the public (and between different sections of the public) could be analysed in a number of different ways. We will argue that it's most appropriate to consider this in psychological terms, but bearing in mind that both the problem itself and any potential solutions are multidimensional and multileveled. It is a global issue, involving different countries and governments (and therefore requiring a consideration of local and global politics), and diverse social groups with different demographics, different patterns of media consumption and different educational levels (and, therefore, a consideration of sociological, economic and educational perspectives), with implications for manufacture and industry (involving a consideration of both economic and international trade). And, of course, it involves *individuals* and their beliefs, values, attitudes and behaviour, which, we would argue, can be thought of as sitting at the centre of everything, with their values and attitudes driving both consumer behaviour and the production of goods.

Psychology may indeed hold the key to many of the more puzzling aspects of our reaction to climate change, but to understand why and how, we will have to venture into the mind of Donald Trump, we will have to consider the gaze fixations of consumers in the first few milliseconds when they look at a product in a supermarket and we will have to analyse how and why human beings use 'lazy' reasoning to arrive at certain types of conclusions and what smoking and climate change have in common. The answer, by the way, is that both are extremely harmful, but for many years, both were the subject of a huge 'scientific debate' (manufactured and paid for) about the real damage they can cause. We will examine how this debate was fuelled and who exactly paid for it. We will venture into the conscious mind of the public and their unconscious mind, and argue that the 'conflict' between these two types of processes might hold the key to many of the recurrent issues in this whole domain (Beattie 2018).

SOME REACTIONS TO THE SCIENCE OF CLIMATE CHANGE

There has been scientific evidence for the role of human activity in producing increased greenhouse gas emissions and climate change for a considerable time. Indeed, as far back as 1896, the Swedish chemist Svante Arrhenius calculated the possible effects of doubling the amount of carbon dioxide on global temperatures. In 1965, President Lyndon B. Johnson's Scientific Advisory Council warned that the constant increase in atmospheric carbon dioxide could 'modify the heat balance of the atmosphere.' In the United Kingdom, the *Stern Review* (conducted by Sir Nicholas Stern, the former chief economist of the World Bank) concluded over a decade ago that 'climate change presents very serious global risks, and it demands an urgent global response.' Stern's conclusion at the time was that 'climate change threatens the basic elements of life for people around the world – access to water, food production, health and use of land and the environment.' Stern also concluded that it is extremely probable that human activity and particularly patterns of consumption and energy use, driven by consumer demand for higher standards of living, are significant factors in the rise of global CO_2 emissions and therefore a major driver of climate change. He argued that 'Emissions have been, and continue to be, driven by economic growth' – a view subsequently supported by the various IPCC reports, as we have seen.

Evidence for climate change has been available for some time, so why has this 'urgent global response' (in Stern's words) not occurred? The IPCC (2015) have argued that we could limit the effects of climate change by changing our individual and collective behaviour. We could fly less, eat less meat, use public transport, cycle or walk, recycle, choose more low carbon products, have shorter showers, waste less food or reduce home energy use. There has been some significant local change but nothing like the 'global response' required to ameliorate the further deleterious effects of climate change.

We are reminded here of a somewhat depressing statistic reported by a leading multinational, Unilever, in their 'Sustainable Living Plan.' In 2013, they outlined how they were going to halve the greenhouse gas impact of their products across the life cycle by 2020. To achieve this goal, they reduced greenhouse gas emissions from their manufacturing chain. They opted for more environmentally friendly sourcing of raw materials, doubled their use of renewable energy and produced concentrated liquids and powders. They reduced greenhouse gas emissions from transport and greenhouse gas emissions from refrigeration. They also restricted employee travel. The result of all of these initiatives was that their 'greenhouse gas footprint impact per consumer. . . . **increased** by around 5% since 2010.' They concluded, 'We have made good progress in those areas under our control but . . . the big challenges are those areas not under our direct control like. . . . **consumer behaviour**' (2013:16; emphasis added). It seems that consumers are not 'getting the message.' They are not opting for the low carbon alternatives in the way envisaged; they are not changing the length of their showers (to reduce energy and water consumption); they are not breaking their high-carbon habits. The question is why?

This failure on the part of the public to change their behaviour is perhaps even more puzzling given that the Department of the Environment, Food and Rural Affairs (DEFRA) in the United Kingdom have repeatedly argued that 'Many people are willing to do a bit more to limit their environmental impact, yet people have a much lower level of understanding about what they can do and what would make a difference.' The Unilever campaign was, of course, designed to help in this regard by making more sustainable products readily available. This led to a number of other government-backed campaigns in the United Kingdom designed to persuade us to change our behaviour – turning off lights when not in use, buying low carbon products, car sharing, etc. These are all relatively clearly defined actions, which could make a significant difference if enough people did them, but the results were disappointing.

Take, for example, the issue of carbon labelling of products to guide consumers towards the more environmentally friendly alternative. Tesco, the UK based retailer, introduced carbon labelling in 2007, aiming to include carbon labels on all of its 70,000 own-brand products. Terry Leahy, CEO of Tesco at that time said, 'The green movement must become a mass movement in green consumption.' To achieve this goal, Leahy argued, 'We must empower everyone – not just the enlightened or the affluent.' But Tesco dropped this plan in 2012; they argued that other supermarkets hadn't joined them in this enterprise and said that the accurate calculation of carbon footprint was slower and far more expensive than originally anticipated. However, in reality, it simply didn't work. And perhaps that could have been anticipated (Beattie 2012). In an experimental situation, the present authors found that when viewing products, people paid very little attention to carbon labels. Using eye tracking to monitor individual gaze fixations on products every 40 milliseconds, we found that in less than 7% of all cases, participants fixate on either the carbon-footprint icon or the accompanying carbon-footprint information in the first five seconds (Beattie et al. 2010). Five seconds is important, because that's the average length of time we view a product before making our choice in a supermarket.

Thus the public in the United Kingdom, in their role as consumers, were not behaving in the way anticipated by both the government and major retailers. There were clearly some important psychological issues here given that people said that they wanted carbon labels on products, but then failed to look at them. This is the kind of issue we will explore in this book, which we started in December 2017. The date could be important – views on climate change do alter depending upon major world events (and the specific weather at any given time, including whether it's snowing or not). It's sometimes critical to put a date stamp on projects, particularly ones like this – projects that affect us all. One day in the future, we might well look back on climate change and wonder what all the fuss was about. The science, after all, was clear and unambiguous. The climate scientists communicated their findings effectively to politicians, policymakers and the public and everyone (more or less at the same time in this ideal scenario) decided that urgent change was required, and, as a result, modified their behaviour at the personal, community, societal and national levels, resulting in a global trend – a seismic shift in attitudes and behaviour. That is one scenario.

Or, *possibly*, one day in the future, we might well look back and wonder why we didn't actually do something about climate change sooner when all the signs were there and clear to see, and now (at this point in the future where some future generations survive) it is simply too late to do anything. The science might have been thought to be clear and unambiguous by *some*, but for whatever set of complex psychological reasons, the message was not received, or it was received but not believed, or it was received and judged to be credible, but we assumed that it wouldn't affect us so we paid scant attention to it in the hurly-burly of our daily lives, or we tried in a small way to make some changes and then we gave up because we concluded that other people were not making the same effort, and we felt foolish.

This is what this book is about – those 'complex psychological reasons,' those psychological factors which may actually be quite simple but incredibly powerful that might be influencing how we respond to climate change at every level in terms of the most basic processes such as attention and perception in terms of our emotional and cognitive responses, in terms of our interpretation and understanding, in terms of our representation and world view, in terms of our willingness to talk and share our views about it to our friends and colleagues (or strangers on a bus) and then further up the chain to our representatives and politicians, all shaping our predisposition to act or not.

So what is the *psychology* of climate change?

2

FAKE NEWS
THE SCIENCE AND POLITICS
OF CLIMATE CHANGE

The year 2017 was in many ways critical for climate change and for us all. On January 20, Donald J. Trump, considered to be a climate change denier, was elected the 45th president of the United States, and later that year, the Fourth National Climate Assessment Report was published by the US Global Change Research Program. Two monumental events for the 'debate' on climate change. Trump said that he would cancel the Paris Climate Agreement within 100 days of taking office; he signed an executive order in March 2017 that reversed the Clean Power Plan that required states to regulate power plants; he described anthropogenic climate change as 'a hoax'.

The Fourth National Climate Assessment Report was yet another report that bolstered the scientific consensus on climate change, but this one was 'the authoritative assessment of the science of climate change,' with a focus on the United States. The fact that the focus was the United States was very important. One major psychological issue with climate change is that it is often perceived to be primarily about other places and other times, and not of direct concern to us living in the here and now. The belief is that it will affect more distant locations (sometimes called 'spatial bias') and not our own, and that it will affect future generations rather than this one (this is called 'temporal bias'). Indeed, in one recent research study, the present authors (Beattie et al, 2017) found that although people (students and employees of a university) thought that they had a 48.1% probability of being *personally* affected by climate change (in other words, the chances are against it), they thought *other people* had a 65.3% probability of being affected by climate change (in other words, the chances are for it). The respondents also reckoned that 82.8% of future generations would be affected (they're really going to get it – probabilistically speaking).

Large sections of the population of the United States seem to assume that they will be immune to the whims of climate change (if it exists at all), and Donald Trump, in his election campaign, tapped into these beliefs, reinforced them and led them. They seem to believe that it doesn't really concern them (except perhaps in terms of what they might have to pay in the light of the Paris Climate Agreement). Many, including the new president himself, described it as a 'hoax,' and this message played very well in his campaign in those states which had been decimated by the decline of the coal industry. He tweeted on November 1, 2012, 'Let's continue to destroy the competitiveness of our factories & manufacturing so we can fight mythical global warming. China is so happy!,' and on February 15, 2015, he tweeted, 'Record low temperatures and massive amounts of snow. Where the hell is GLOBAL WARMING?'

'Where the hell is global warming when you need it?' became a recurrent slogan (from a tweet from Donald Trump on May 14, 2013). Perhaps the man on the bus had seen the tweets; perhaps he didn't need to.

'Right here, right now,' was the answer from the Fourth National Climate Assessment Report. This report read:

> Global annually averaged surface air temperature has increased by about 1.8° F (1.0° C) over the last 115 years (1901–2016). This period is now the warmest in the history of modern civilisation . . . it is extremely likely that human activities, especially emissions of greenhouse gases, are the dominant cause of the

observed warming since the mid-20th century . . . in addition to warming, many other aspects of global climate are changing, primarily in response to human activities. Thousands of studies conducted by researchers from around the world have documented changes in surface, atmospheric and oceanic temperatures; melting glaciers; diminishing snow cover; shrinking sea ice; rising sea levels; ocean acidification; and increasing atmospheric water vapor.

(USGCRP, 2017: 10)

The upshot of these changes for the United States are well documented in the report; it explains how there has been an increase in extreme weather events with heavy rainfall increasing in intensity and frequency, a higher frequency of heatwaves, an increase in the frequency of large forest fires in the western United States in Alaska and reduced snowpack affecting water resources in the western United States. The report warns that 'assuming no change to current water resources management, chronic, long-duration hydrological drought is increasingly possible before the end of this century.'

This is a balanced and authoritative scientific assessment, but science, of course, works on the principles of scientific testing and prediction and probability. Very few things in life are actually certain. So the report says, 'It is extremely likely that human activities, especially emissions of greenhouse gases are the dominant cause of the observed warming since the mid-20th century.' Science is based on probabilities, and the report, therefore, goes to the trouble of explaining these key probabilistic terms with a glossary. They explain that 'likelihood' is the 'chance of occurrence of an effect or impact based on measures of uncertainty expressed probabilistically.' They also explain that 'extremely likely' means that it has a 95%–100% chance of occurring. Scientists understand the full significance of this. But, of course, critics, cynics, extreme optimists, those with a vested interest, the president of the United States (at this time in our history) seize on these probabilistic terms. 'It's not certain,' they say. 'Why should we change our behaviour, our values, our culture, our economic position in the world for something that is just *likely*? Okay, extremely likely. This doesn't mean that it's going to happen *for sure*. If we change our coal and oil industries, I'll tell you what, we're going to surrender our economic position to China, and that is *for sure*.' The year 2017 was a year of non-science, and 'fake news' and discussions that weren't.

Towards the close of the year, things started heating up. President Trump was on vacation, again, at his Mar-a-Lago resort in West Palm Beach, Florida, for an 11-day Christmas break. The sun was shining. They don't call it the Sunshine State for nothing. On the first morning of his vacation, he was predictably enough back on his own golf course. It seems that this was his 85th day on a golf course since becoming president, according to NBC News. Whilst the rest of the world was worrying about the ongoing nuclear stand-off with North Korea's Kim Jong-un and President Trump's recent boasts about the size of his nuclear button ('I too have a Nuclear Button, but it is a much bigger & more powerful one than his, and my Button works!'), the president reassured us that he would be 'working very hard' on preparing a 2018 agenda that would include both infrastructure plans to 'Make America Great' again and unspecified 'actions' against North Korea. 'I'll be working very hard,' he said again. We were urged not to worry by this 'stable genius' of a president, as he was soon to describe himself – a stable genius who had everything under control.

CONSISTENCY AND INCONSISTENCY

But consistency, of course, was never his strong point. In October 2014, President Trump tweeted: 'Can you believe that, with all of the problems and difficulties facing the US, President Obama spent the day playing golf.' Before entering the White House, at a campaign rally, he assured the American people that 'I'm going to be working for you, I'm not going to have time to go play golf.' But that was then. He played three times as much golf as his predecessor Barack Obama and that other great golfing president George W. Bush, who stopped playing altogether in 2003 in response to widespread criticism about his conspicuous leisure time during the Iraq War. President Trump enjoyed the golf in the bright sunshine with a few golfing pros and the odd senator. Perfect. The weather did everything that was expected of it that Christmas and New Year. And not just in Florida. A cold snap hit the north-east coast of the United States. Dogs froze to death in their kennels. Could life get any better for Donald J. Trump?

'In the East, it could be the COLDEST New Year's Eve on record. Perhaps we could use a little bit of that good old Global Warming that our Country, but not other countries, was going to pay TRILLIONS OF DOLLARS to protect against. Bundle up!' he tweeted gleefully on the December 28.

Trump had always been a climate change denier, although 'always,' again, is a relative term here. In 2009, he was a signatory on an open letter which had been addressed to President Obama and published in the *New York Times* that encouraged positive governmental action on climate change. But his subsequent climate change denial was a big part of his 'Make America Great' campaign. Climate change was a Chinese conspiracy to damage American industry. It was a total hoax-fake news. The message played well to the masses, particularly in those states whose heavy industry had been most affected by foreign competition. In December 2017, the Trump administration dropped climate change from a list of global threats in the new national security strategy that the president unveiled. Then the cold snap occurred. Just look at the news to see what happening in the north-east states of the great USA, he was saying.

And then it just got a whole lot better. In the New Year, Florida had its first snowfall in nearly three decades. Frozen iguanas were dropping from the trees. Homeowners in the Sunshine State were warned to leave them alone until they defrosted. One could even imagine Trump sticking a picture of a frozen iguana on his laptop. The most powerful man in the world had evidence that climate change was a total hoax. That iguana did it for him. You can't fake a frozen iguana. When you have to defrost iguanas in Florida, that tells you all you need to know about global warming, he perhaps thought.

President Trump seems to have inconsistent views on climate change (and inconsistent views on so much else besides) and is prone to serious conceptual confusions – for example, about the difference between 'climate' (the bigger picture across time) and 'weather' (the smaller, more localised picture, with a whole series of fluctuations and changes). On November 1, 2011, he tweeted 'It snowed over 4 inches this past weekend in New York City. It is still October. So much for Global Warming.' Indeed, he is so confused on this most basic issue that Kendra Pierre-Louis, writing in the *New York Times* on December 28, 2017, thought it necessary to offer him an analogy in terms that he might understand. She wrote,

> Weather is how much money you have in your pocket today, whereas climate is your net worth. A billionaire who has forgotten his wallet one day is not poor, any more than a poor person who lands a windfall of several hundred dollars is suddenly rich. What matters is what happens over the long term.

Trump on his golf course without his wallet was still the billionaire he always was, and the drinks for his buddies were still on him.

In her *New York Times* piece, Pierre-Louis moved from bulging wallets to melting snowmen and explained to the president and others who were also reassured by the cold snap that

> while climate scientists expect that the world could warm, on average, roughly 2 to 7 degrees Fahrenheit by the end of the century – depending on how quickly greenhouse-gas emissions rise – they don't expect that to mean the end of winter altogether. Record low temperatures will still occur; they'll just become rarer over time.

There will always be snowmen, she was saying; they'll just be rarer.

But, of course, there may be more to the psychology of climate change, and climate change denial in particular, than mere political (or financial) expediency, and some basic conceptual confusions about weather and climate, including personality. President Trump, of course, has a very distinctive personality. Many have commented on this. Indeed, so distinctive that 60,000 mental health professionals, including prominent members of the American Psychological Association, broke with tradition (and the ethical rules governing their profession) to offer a clinical diagnosis of the president. He clearly appears to be highly egocentric and narcissistic, a man who routinely attempts to gain personal advantage in the micro-politics of everyday interaction. He has even managed to turn the handshake – a universal symbol of equality and cooperation which dates back at least as far as Ancient Greece – into something competitive and self-serving. His 'clasp-and-yank' handshake has taken many of its recipients by surprise (Beattie 2016). But he's not just an egocentric narcissist, extremely sensitive to any criticism or apparent snub, who tries to gain an advantage in all aspects of life; he is also undoubtedly an optimist, as are many successful entrepreneurs (see Beattie 2017). Indeed, Crane and Crane (2007) identified 'optimism' and 'work ethic' as the two most important characteristics that distinguish successful entrepreneurs. Of the two, optimism was the more important. Optimists tend to look on the bright side of life, but from a psychological point of view, the most important thing about optimists is that they take credit for the good things that happen to them in their lives but don't blame themselves for the bad things that occur. They seem to think intuitively that the negative things in life tend to be the result of many factors (other people, the situation, the time of day, the economy), and they make their attribution accordingly. They are not so analytic, or thoughtful, when it comes to the positive events they encounter ('Of course, the project was successful. I was in charge!'). They think that good things are just around the corner and as a consequence tend to be very resilient. Optimists bounce back after failure. It may be recalled that Trump declared himself bankrupt four times before achieving billionaire status.

This all seems very positive, and Martin Seligman in *Authentic Happiness* has argued that optimism is very important for health and well-being. But there is always the danger of being overly optimistic, of thinking naïvely that everything will be okay in the end, of not seeing the warning signs about the economy, world terrorism or climate change, as the American author Barbara Ehrenreich noted in her book *Smile or Die: How Positive Thinking Fooled America and the World*. This over-optimism may well influence how Donald Trump processes information, as we will see in Chapter 4, and is particularly important for how he might attend to and process bad news, such as the scientific consensus on climate change. By analysing dispositional optimists (such as Donald Trump), we may learn a great deal about the role of cognitive biases in the development of people's views on climate change.

We have already mentioned the apparent vacillation of Trump on climate change, but it is a particular sort of vacillation with two mutually contradictory viewpoints held with apparent equal force and conviction. But which statement or action represents his real *underlying* attitude to climate change and which is said for political effect? Was it his attack on Obama in the case of the pro-climate change letter to the *New York Times* – does he really deep down inside believe in climate change? Or was his labelling of climate change as 'a hoax' indicative of his genuine belief? Can we, in fact, distinguish expressed and consciously held attitudes from something that runs a bit deeper like implicit and unconscious attitudes that are not readily available to introspection? Do underlying implicit attitudes actually exist? And if they do, how can we measure them? How important might these be to the discourses of climate change and to our everyday behaviour?

Some of these considerations might help us uncover and explain aspects of the psychology of climate change and that curious state of affairs where the great climate scientists of the world are jumping up and down and warning of an approaching apocalypse whilst huge swathes of the population stay calm, relaxed and sanguine in their thinking and approach.

Donald Trump is an odd sort of president, and one day, we will surely look back and wonder how his transformation into the most important person on the planet could ever have happened. But he is an odd president at a critical and dangerous time for us all, both in terms of world events (North Korea, Iran, Israel, Russia) and climate change. He keeps repeating the same messages over and over again – 'Crooked Hillary,' 'Lock Her Up,' 'Fake News,' 'Total Hoax' – based on that simple advertising proposition of repetition, repetition, repetition. And (if the truth be told) it is sometimes hard not to look at an image of Hillary Clinton without that repetitively associated word 'crooked' popping into our heads. So it might well be in the future with 'climate change' and 'hoax.' That is a major fear.

We can learn a lot from Donald Trump about expressed attitudes and implicit attitudes, about conceptual confusions, about cognitive biases, about over-optimism, about associative networks that operate below the level of consciousness, about repetition and the mind, about the role of images in thinking, about communication and conflicted thoughts, about psychological flaws that we need to correct. That is why we have used Donald Trump as a peg for this little book on the psychology of climate change. A peg, after all, is a very vivid image and, to our minds, preferable to a dead iguana, at least in terms of its effect.

WORLDS APART

President Trump is also a good bookmark – a reminder that we all don't think alike when it comes to climate change. There is clearly a great divide between scientists and the public generally on climate change, as we have seen. But there is an equally significant divide amongst the public themselves, between believers and non-believers, between Republicans and Democrats, between certain political parties in the United Kingdom, between the right-wing and left-wing press and between Donald Trump and Al Gore-the two great icons on each side of the climate change debate. Both Trump and Gore, it must be said, have used language hardly appropriate for building consensus and understanding amongst the public. Trump's tweets speak for themselves, of course. Al Gore, unfortunately, has used equally inflammatory language. In a 2011 *Rolling Stone* interview, the former Vice President said, 'In one corner of the ring are Science and Reason. In the other corner: Poisonous Polluters and Right-wing Ideologues.' This is hardly the kind of language we need to bridge this cultural divide and promote a shared understanding.

There are clearly deeply held cultural, political and religious beliefs that divide the two groups. It's not just a question of science and scientific knowledge. This point was recently made by Stephen Pinker in conversation with Bill Gates who said,

> One of the biggest enemies of reason is tribalism. When people subscribe to an ideology, they suck up evidence that supports their preconceptions and filter out evidence that goes against them. Contrary to the belief of most scientists that denial of climate change is an effect of scientific illiteracy, it is not at all correlated with scientific literacy. People who believe in man-made climate change don't know any more about climate or science than those who deny it. It's almost perfectly correlated with left-wing versus right-wing orientation. And a move towards greater rationality would unbundle them and let evidence inform what the optimal policies ought to be.
>
> (Reported in the *New York Times* January 27, 2018).

The statistics on this divide fuelled by ideological position are striking. Andrew Hoffman in his book *How Culture Shapes the Climate Change Debate* reports that in 1997, 47% of Republicans and 46% of Democrats thought that climate change was already happening, in other words virtually identical percentages. By 2008, the figures had diverged dramatically, with fewer Republicans holding this view (down to 41%) but with far more Democrats than previously expressing this position (up to 76%). By 2013, the respective figures were further apart still: 50% and 88%, respectively. Hoffman says that the cause of this polarisation on ideological grounds after 1997 was the Kyoto Protocol, which was the first international agreement to reduce greenhouse gas emissions which was supported by the Clinton administration. Media attention on the political and economic implications of climate change rose dramatically in the years following. McCright and Dunlap (2011) reported that there were 166 documents critical of the science of climate change in 1997 alone. One hundred and seven climate change denial books were published between 1989 and 2010. Most of these, according to Hoffman, were linked to conservative think tanks, and somewhat tellingly, 90% did not go through a peer-review process (the very bedrock of science itself).

Hoffman's book reminds us of the complexity of this whole issue and how economic (and political) factors and psychology are intimately connected, and that psychology, of course, is part of the world and not separate from it. The Kyoto Protocol to reduce greenhouse gas emissions had major implications for the energy sector and industry in the United States, and a counter-campaign was mounted. This brings us into murkier waters where we will swim in Chapter 6 when we consider how the science linking smoking and cancer, and linking human activity and climate change were both turned into 'scientific debates,' which allowed both viewpoints to flourish and stay literally worlds apart.

3

OUR RATIONAL AND IRRATIONAL SELVES

AUTOMATIC VERSUS RATIONAL RESPONSES

Science points to certain inescapable conclusions in the case of climate change, but a large proportion of the general population seems not to accept these conclusions, nor act on them. So what is the psychology behind this? Can we read people's minds to work out what is going on here? We want to argue that this is much more difficult than it might at first appear because human beings don't actually have a mind - they have two! Psychology suggests that people have two distinct cognitive systems, each with its own properties and mode of operation. One of these systems is conscious (what we think of as our 'mind,' in expressions such as 'I've changed my mind'). The other system is not conscious and not open to introspection – it's hidden but extremely important in guiding our actions. The Nobel Laureate Daniel Kahneman (2011) calls these systems 'System 1' (the fast, automatic and largely unconscious system) and 'System 2' (the slower, more deliberate and reflective conscious system). This could be the reason why so many initiatives (like carbon labelling) have failed. They made the wrong basic assumption about human beings: they assumed that people knew their own minds, and they didn't realise that there was another process at work.

Take a very simple example (from Kahneman's book): imagine looking at an angry face – as quickly as you recognise the gender of the person or the colour of the person's hair, you have decoded the facial expression. This is System 1 thinking – it's automatic, unconscious and fast. Driving along a quiet road, responding to a simple message, recognising an advert are all examples of System 1 in operation. A multiplication task, on the other hand, is much slower and more deliberate; it requires effort and is conscious. Try multiplying 13 by 87 and you'll see what we mean. This is System 2 thinking in Kahneman's terminology, as is looking for a friend in a crowd, careful parking, comparing two products for value, etc. In everyday life, System 1 is always active, dealing with many of the routine aspects of everyday life (including the decoding of emotional expression). Kahneman characterises System 1 as a 'workaholic' and System 2 as sometimes a bit lazy ('harsh . . . but not unfair,' according to Kahneman, 2011: 46).

System 1 often jumps rapidly to conclusions, but System 2 doesn't always check the validity of the conclusions, even when it would be easy to do this. The well-known example he gives is 'a bat and ball cost one pound ten pence, the bat costs one pound more than the ball. How much does the ball cost?' Eighty per cent of university students say 10 pence. This feels right but is incorrect. The correct answer, of course, is 5 pence. System 2 often endorses what feels right without going to the trouble of checking.

The two systems work on different principles. System 1 works on the principle of associative activation:

> ideas that have been evoked trigger many other ideas, in a spreading cascade of activity in your brain. The essential feature of this complex set of mental events is its coherence. Each element is connected, and each supports and strengthens the others.
>
> (Kahneman, 2011: 51)

System 2 uses more propositional and logical reasoning.

Kahneman uses the example of 'bananas – vomit' to show how System 1 works in terms of this pattern of spreading activation. Our minds automatically assume a causal connection between the two words, producing within us an emotional response, and changes the state of our memory so that we are now more likely to recognise and respond to objects and concepts associated with sickness and nausea. We are, for example, more likely to complete the frame 's-ck' as 'sick' rather than as 'sock' or 'suck,' having been unconsciously primed with the paired concepts of 'bananas' and 'vomit,' all because of this associative 'machine' underpinning System 1 thinking. Kahneman argues that as human beings, we do not necessarily understand the causes and operations of our own cognitions and behaviours because of this fundamental division in our cognitive processes.

> When we think of ourselves, we identify with System 2, the conscious, reasoning self that has beliefs, makes choices, and decides what to think about and what to do. Although System 2 believes itself to be where the action is, the automatic System 1 . . . is effortlessly originating impressions and feelings that are the main sources of the explicit beliefs and deliberate choices of System 2.
>
> (2011: 21)

The media uses the 'bananas – vomit' paradigm every day in every article, editorial, comment, alignment of image and text; it works on this process of spreading activation. We are then primed to recognise new information, to fill in the blanks, to jump to conclusions. 'Climate change – hoax' or alternatively 'climate change – global catastrophe,' which as we saw in Chapter 2 are played out and repeated in different media (including the Twittersphere of Donald J. Trump), and set up different patterns of spreading activation. These associations in System 1 then influence what we endorse in lazy System 2. We often jump to conclusions without examining the evidence because of the activation of System 1 and its emotional undercurrents. This distinction between two types of cognitive processes in everyday cognition may help us understand some of the cognitive biases that we are clearly susceptible to.

Paul Slovic and colleagues (2002) have described one very significant bias called the 'affect heuristic,' where people allow their likes and dislikes to determine their beliefs about the world. 'Affect' is used by Slovic and his colleagues to describe a feeling state either with or without consciousness. They write, '*Affective responses* occur rapidly and automatically – note how quickly you sense the feelings associated with the stimulus words *treasure* or *hate*. We argue that reliance on such feelings can be characterized as the affect heuristic' (2002: 397). This idea had been discussed previously by Zajonc (1980), who suggested that affective reactions are the automatic responses that guide subsequent information processing. This is essentially the operation of System 1, which in many domains has an affective basis. As Slovic says, 'Although analysis is certainly important in some decision-making circumstances, reliance on affect and emotion is a quicker, easier and more efficient way to navigate in a complex, uncertain and sometimes dangerous world.' Emotion then can direct your search for, and processing of, relevant information. In domains where there is a lot of information (like climate change), and we don't have to time to read it all, your emotional response can direct you to focus on certain bits of information rather than others. Your emotional attitudes to exercise (positive!), genetically modified foods (negative!) or climate change mitigation strategies (positive!) affect what you attend to. Your emotional response then determines your beliefs about their benefits and risks. If you like exercise, then you probably believe that the risks are low, and the benefits are very high. When you are presented with the relevant information, you process it and recall it in a biased way.

One might imagine that the conscious and rational System 2 often has the 'ability to resist the suggestion of System 1, slow things down, and impose logical analysis. Self-criticism is one of the functions of System 2' (Kahneman 2011: 103). However, in the light of the work on the affect heuristic and attitudes, Kahneman concludes,

> System 2 is more of an apologist for the emotions of System 1 than a critic of those emotions – an endorser rather than an enforcer. Its search for information and arguments is mostly

constrained to information that is consistent with existing beliefs, not with an intention to examine them. An active, coherence-seeking System 1 suggests solutions to an undemanding System 2.

(Kahneman 2011: 103–104)

This is called the confirmation bias. We seek information that supports what we already believe and that is concurrent with our feelings about it.

Kahneman's work offers us a coherent framework for thinking about biases and how they might operate in any context, including climate change. It emphasises the importance and primacy of our emotional responses in determining our rationally expressed beliefs, and offers a theoretical perspective on the very different processes that underpin our everyday cognitions. The associative processes of spreading activation are so significant because they are the processes that are used by the workaholic System 1, that hidden, unconscious system that determines so many of our core beliefs as endorsed (rather than tested) by System 2. We may like to think that we are the embodiment of System 2, that we are that rational, reflective system that thinks carefully about the world before making any decision, but we would be badly mistaken.

THE AFFECT HEURISTIC IN OPERATION

You don't have to look far in your own experience to find some personal evidence of this. One of the authors (the particular account should identify which one) tells the following story. It's a story about a lecture on the dangers of drugs back in his youth, but much more than that, it's a story about the affect heuristic in operation.

"I was a teenager at the time growing up in the damp, grey streets of the Belfast of the Troubles. Life was disjointed and fractured. As a teenager my social life was restricted to the streets around me – endless hours of hanging about 'the corner.' The press called my streets 'murder triangle.'

"But, of course, I realised that there was a life somewhere out there better than this, but it was too far away to glimpse or touch. The world of the NME, the News of the World with stories about the sordid goings on of rock stars, images of jeans tucked into green boots, Biba, fast cars. The swings in our local park were chained up on a Sunday lest we enjoy ourselves on the Lord's Day.

"It was a Friday in my local youth club that he came to talk to us. We were all boys. I remember that; it was a funny sort of youth club, and we were asked to pull our chairs out into neat rows in front of the speaker. There was an opening introduction then a slideshow with images of pills and plants, a glossary of terms, some of which I had heard before, many of which I had not: amphetamine, speed, pep pills, black bombers, dexies, black beauties, black-and-white minstrels LSD, purple haze, yellow sunshine, blue heaven, sugar cubes, marijuana, dope, grass, cocaine, coke, Californian Cornflakes.

"From the opening slide, I was captivated. It was as if the drugs were jumping off the slides, almost three-dimensional in their appearance. I don't think that I once blinked in case I missed something. Things were being revealed to me, to us all; we were all drug and pop culture virgins. I had a series of agonising shocks of recognition and clarity. 'Purple haze, all in my brain' wasn't a song about pollution and traffic jams, and the way that street lights can play odd tricks with your vision when the shipyard was closing and the streets were packed.

"I was hooked. Hooked on the glamour and the glitz, hooked on the terms, with their implicit connotations of something better – 'black beauties,' 'yellow sunshine,' 'Californian Cornflakes.' Hooked on finding the way out from a world where the swings never moved on a Sunday. And when the slides showed close-ups of black bombers, I realised that my rusted bathroom cabinet with the shaky mottled glass door pinned to the wall in our kitchen (because we didn't have a bathroom nor an inside toilet) was full of drugs, full of black bombers, used by my mother as slimming pills. That night, my friends and I took drugs for the first time and gabbled away outside the chip shop for hours. It probably wasn't that much fun, but we all felt different and separate from everyone else, empowered in a curious sort of way".

This, of course, is just an anecdote, a single case study about the disaffected youth of Belfast one rainy Friday night a long time ago, but it perhaps reminds us of the challenge that behaviour change campaigns face. Get it wrong and you can get it badly wrong. You can actually make things worse than if you hadn't bothered. The speaker that night with his slides and his spiel did not have a clear understanding of our lives, nor of our social situation. When you communicate, you need a clear model of the audience, their mental state, their needs and their aspirations. He had no such model. You have to be able to read other minds. He couldn't. You also need the right approach. He went for a cognitive, rational approach and explained patiently to us that drugs were dangerous. But this meant very little to us. Going for a pint of milk was dangerous where we lived. Telling us that drugs affected the biochemistry of the brain cut no ice either, a night outside the chip shop with the drive-by shootings and then the backfiring cars messed up the biochemistry of your brain. We all knew that. We all had friends who had cracked up after hours spent hanging about the corner doing nothing. None of them needed drugs to help them along. And the presenter underestimated the great emotional pull drugs had for us corner boys, the emotional connotations, fashion, rebellion, life in your own hands, not the hands of others, living dangerously because you wanted to, not because others wanted you to.

This great emotional pull influenced what I noticed and remembered about the message. 'No more dangerous than an Outward Bound Weekend,' he said about the slimming pills. That's what I focussed in on that night, and that's what I remember after all these years. Emotion guides cognition. System 1 with associated emotional markers guides and directs System 2. It affected what I heard, what I remembered and what I repeated to my friends ('No more dangerous than an Outward Bound Weekend,' I explained endlessly). Funnily enough, that's what we all remembered.

THE EMOTIONAL AND THE CONCEPTUAL SYSTEM

Antonio Damasio has reported that in normal people, activation of the emotional system precedes activation of any conceptual or reasoning system and, perhaps as importantly, that the two systems are separate. He demonstrated this with a very simple gambling experiment (Bechara et al. 1997). Sitting in front of the participant is four decks of cards. In the participant's hands is $2,000 to gamble with. The task is to turn over one card at a time to win the maximum amount of money; with each card, the participant would either win some money or lose some money. In the case of two of the decks, the rewards are great ($100), but so too are the penalties. If you play either of these two decks for any period of time, you end up losing money. On the other hand, if you concentrate on selecting cards from the other two decks, you get smaller rewards ($50) but also smaller penalties, and you end up winning money in the course of the game. But these 'reward/penalty' factors are unknown to the participant at the start of the game.

What Damasio found with people playing this game was that, after encountering a few losses, normal participants generated skin conductance responses (a sign of autonomic arousal) before selecting a card from the 'bad deck,' and they also started to avoid the decks associated with bad losses. In other words, they showed a distinct emotional response to the bad decks, even before they had a conceptual understanding of the nature of the decks and long before they could explain what was going on. They started to avoid the bad decks on the basis of their emotional response.

Damasio also found that patients with damage to a particular area of the brain called the ventromedial prefrontal cortex failed to generate a skin conductance response before selecting cards from the bad deck and did not avoid the decks with large losses. Patients with damage to this part of the brain could not generate the anticipatory skin conductance response and could not avoid the bad decks, even though they conceptually understood the difference in the nature of the decks before them. In the words of the authors, 'The patients failed to act according to their correct conceptual knowledge.' In other words,

Damasio and his colleagues demonstrated that 'in normal individuals, non-conscious biases guide behaviour before conscious knowledge does. Without the help of such biases, overt knowledge may be insufficient to ensure advantageous behavior.' In normal people, activation of the emotional system precedes activation of the conceptual system, and we now know the neural connection between these two systems is located in the ventromedial prefrontal cortex.

SOCIAL BIASES AND CLIMATE CHANGE

But there are other biases in addition to the affect heuristic and the confirmation bias. Ross (1977) considered how people reasoned about their social worlds. Are people good intuitive psychologists, as many of us like to think, carefully considering the behavioural data of everyday life and the antecedents of action to arrive at conclusions about why they (and others) behave the way they do? The answer was that we might think of ourselves as rational agents and good observers of people, keen on analysis and reflection, but in reality, we are subject to a whole series of biases that affect what we see, how we interpret it and the conclusions we draw. For example, we tend to view our own behaviour as being appropriate in any social situation and see behaviour different from our own as both inappropriate and more indicative of underlying disposition. We assume that it tells us more about the other person. We also often suffer from a false consensus effect, believing that our own behaviour is more common than it really is and that the majority of people share our world views, our attitudes, our preferences, even our emotional states. For example, people who suffer from depression reckon that 55.1% of people generally suffer from depression (Ross 1977). 'Put more money into mental health,' they say, 'it's an epidemic.' Those who do not suffer from depression reckon that only 39.2% suffer from depression. 'It's bad,' they say, 'but it's not that bad.'

Ross never considered climate change, but he did consider beliefs in the possibility of a nuclear war occurring. Those who believed that nuclear war was inevitable reckoned that 58.8% of people generally thought that it would occur. Those who didn't think that it would occur reckoned that 31.2% of people thought that it would happen. The false consensus effect amplifies the fear of nuclear war, or the complacency about it, depending on your point of view. If you believe that a nuclear war is inevitable, and you think that most people also think this, it may mobilise you towards certain actions, not all of which are benign.

And so with climate change. There are climate change believers ('everybody knows that we're heading towards a catastrophe') and climate change deniers ('what's all the fuss about? There is a small cabal of politically motivated campaigners out for their own ends'). Both groups then make more extreme and confident judgements about the dispositions of the 'other' (the believers are perceived as 'Democrats in the US, liberal elite, left-wing environmentalists, left leaning, possibly socialist, certainly anti-capitalism, agitators'; the deniers are perceived as 'Republicans in the US, right-wing, conservative, anti-scientific, religious values doctrinaire'), and you can see how this might play out with climate change, as with so much else. It's not just that there is a schism in beliefs, rather there is a schism bolstered by a false consensus and more extreme thinking about the 'other.'

Leviston and Walker (2012) asked over 5,000 Australians to describe their own opinion on climate change using various categories (including 'don't know,' 'not happening,' 'a natural occurrence' and 'human-induced'). They also asked them to estimate what proportion of the population fell into each of these categories. They found that over 90% of their participants believed that climate change was happening with just over half (50.4%) accepting that human beings were responsible. Only 5% reported that it was not happening. They also found clear evidence of false consensus effects with all groups overestimating the proportion of people who shared their view. Those who didn't think that the climate was changing reckoned that over 40% of Australians shared that view!

So where does this false consensus effect come from? The false consensus effect is a form of social bias linked to other cognitive and motivational biases. Firstly, it arises from the necessarily biased sample of our own personal social experiences. Ross argues that we tend to mix with people who share similar views to ourselves, and therefore we don't sample representative behaviours, beliefs or attitudes to arrive at an accurate conclusion. When we are asked to think of how common a behaviour or belief is, we draw upon the social data that comes rapidly to mind, be it what our friends have just said about climate change, or images that they've shared with us on social media (a frozen iguana versus a stranded polar bear, for example). This also affects our judgements about risk and our perception that climate change is either very risky or a total hoax. Tversky and Kahneman (1973) have called this the 'availability heuristic'; we base our judgements on probability and risk on the data that is easiest to recall. Vivid images on social media will have a powerful effect on our judgement (this outweighs probabilistic statistical information in science reports or in the media). Secondly, there is a good deal of ambiguity in everyday social life which allows for different interpretations depending on our underlying knowledge, attitudes and beliefs. There is a degree of 'cherry-picking' of the evidence that supports our underlying beliefs through the confirmation bias. George Marshall, in his book *Don't Even Think About It*, says that this operates at all kinds of levels, even in terms of the perception of the weather itself. He writes,

> When asked about recent weather in their own area, people who are already disposed to believe in climate change will tend to say it's been warmer. People who are unconvinced about climate change will say it's been colder. Farmers in Illinois, invited to report their recent experiences of the weather, emphasised or played down extreme events depending on whether or not they accepted climate change.

(2014: 15)

So the same basic pattern of weather can be used to support one view or the opposite view with a cherry-picking of the data and the (often implicit) comparison data ('colder' or 'warmer' are, after all, comparative terms). Thirdly, Ross argues that the false consensus bias is a form of ego-defence. We protect ourselves (and justify our actions and beliefs) by overestimating how common our own characteristic behaviours and attitudes are. Behaviours different from our own are perceived as 'uncommon, deviant and inappropriate,' and much more revealing about underlying disposition.

Hopefully, it should be clearer now how a description of the underlying systems of cognition, as outlined by Kahneman, can help us understand the nature of the cognitive biases when it comes to climate change. We may think of ourselves as rational creatures, reflecting on information to reach conclusions, but we need to remember the workaholic (and hidden) System 1 beavering away, offering us emotionally laden impressions to allow us to jump quickly to decisions, bypassing rational thought. Remember what Kahneman said about System 2; it is an 'endorser' rather than an 'enforcer.' We then cherry-pick information to justify our actions (if we have to) as the confirmation bias takes over. You can also see how these systems contribute to the *conflict* over climate change. We are not good intuitive psychologists; we don't sample the data; we mix with people like ourselves – people who share our views of the world. We end up with a false consensus. We're not just right; we are the moral majority; we are the norm, and there's nothing strange or distinctive about us (just about the ones who disagree).

But there is another very significant bias when it comes to climate change, which may be particularly relevant to our lack of action to remedy this issue, and that is the 'optimism bias.' How do we stay so sanguine in the light of this existential threat? How do (most) people stay so optimistic in the light of all of that scientific evidence? We wanted to understand the processes that may underpin this bias. So we presented the scientific arguments about climate change (and the counter-arguments) to people and analysed their gaze fixations millisecond by millisecond. The results, it has to be said, were very revealing.

4

SEE NO EVIL
HOW DO WE STAY SO OPTIMISTIC?

Information about the science of climate change is readily available and has been reproduced endlessly in newspapers, television and film. But it is not good news; it is highly threatening and very negative, affecting directly the emotional state and mood (Beattie 2011; Beattie, Sale and McGuire 2011). But what happens if people avoid seeing this information? And what we mean here is automatically tuning out, rather than (say) not buying a cinema ticket to go and watch Al Gore's *An Inconvenient Truth*. What happens if people attend instead to arguments *against* climate change (which, by definition, present a much rosier picture of both the present and of the future – 'there is actually significant doubt about anthropogenic climate change and your current lifestyle is totally acceptable')?

There is evidence from other domains which suggests that some people do have a bias in both processing and explaining positive and negative information, and that this bias is linked to 'dispositional optimism.' Dispositional optimism 'refers to generalised outcome expectancies that good things, rather than bad things, will happen; pessimism refers to the tendency to expect negative outcomes in the future' (Taylor 1998). Seligman (2002) has argued that optimists and pessimists differ in terms of one basic psychological feature – namely, attributional style, as we saw in Chapter 2. However, there may be another psychological factor that also distinguishes optimists and pessimists. Attributional style is cognitive reasoning about events, but what about the perception of any such events in the first place? Could this also distinguish optimists and pessimists? Isaacowitz (2006) has argued that dispositional optimism affects basic perceptual processes and that optimists quite literally look on the bright side of life. He used an eye-tracking procedure to investigate this, tracking individual gaze fixations, when participants looked at images of skin cancer, line drawings with the same shape as the cancer images, and neutral faces. He selected images of skin cancer because they are clearly 'negative' images, being both unpleasant and graphic. He found that young adults high in dispositional optimism fixated less on these skin cancer images than their less optimistic peers (Isaacowitz 2006: 68). In other words, Isaacowitz claims that the adult gaze preferences 'towards positive and away from negative images suggest that gaze patterns may reflect an underlying motivation to regulate emotions and to feel good.' (Isaacowitz 2006: 69). Luo and Isaacowitz (2007) also reported negative relationships between dispositional optimism and eye gaze to both negative and neutral text about skin cancer. The negative correlation suggests that optimists may read information about a negative topic more quickly than do pessimists. Other research has shown that individual differences in mood are associated with attentional bias to certain stimuli. Individuals suffering from anxiety or depression have attentional biases towards negative information (Mathews and MacLeod 2002). Attentional bias to certain affective stimuli appears to be motivated by the need to self-regulate emotion, or maintain one's positive mood state.

Therefore, according to Isaacowitz (2006), Seligman (2002) and others, optimists have distinct cognitive 'strategies,' involving both attention and attributional reasoning, for staying optimistic. At the level of the individual, this might be a very good thing, because there is evidence that optimists live longer and healthier lives than pessimists (Seligman 2002), and, consequently, using a range of techniques, people have been trained to become more optimistic. This is the basis not only of much of cognitive behavioural therapy but also a veritable self-help industry.

However, this may not have been as good for society (or the world) as a whole. Barbara Ehrenreich (2009) has argued that these high levels of optimism have 'undermined preparedness' to deal with real threats, including 9/11, the economic bubble bursting, world terrorism, etc. 'The truth is that Americans had been working hard for decades to school themselves in the techniques of positive thinking, and these included the reflexive capacity for dismissing disturbing news.' (Ehrenreich 2009:10). The economic crisis, she argues, is a case in point ('imagining an invulnerable nation and an ever-booming economy-there was simply no ability or inclination to imagine the worst' (Ehrenreich 2009:11). Ehrenreich has argued that the problem was that 'professional optimists dominated the world of economic commentary' (Ehrenreich 2009:181) and that some people who had managed to anticipate the forthcoming economic disaster 'had been under pressure over the years to improve their attitude.' This is the downside of optimism: the fact that people may not notice warning signs that are available and that a focus on the negative is actually an important aspect of human survival.

One very significant question is whether optimists may be missing some of the crucial signs of climate change because they are avoiding seeing them. There is some evidence of this. For example, individuals who reported feeling concerned, worried and anxious about climate change were less likely to avoid information about climate change, and more likely seek out such information (Yang and Kahlor 2012). Beattie et al. (2010) found that participants in an experimental setting sometimes fixate early on the carbon footprint labels of products such as low energy light bulbs, where, of course, the information about carbon footprint is positive, but not on the carbon footprint labels of products where the information is higher (such as detergent).

However, there is one counter study here. Beattie and McGuire (2011) did not find any evidence of an attentional bias in optimists away from negative iconic images of climate change, when these were presented on a computer screen alongside positive images of nature and images of neutral objects. Indeed, the negative images of climate change were fixated more by the optimists. However, these iconic images of climate change may have differed in other ways from the rest of the images. The iconic images of climate change, polar bears on ice floes, Manhattan under water, deserts or a tsunami crashing against a tropical shore might have conjured up images of challenge and adventure rather than just straightforward negative affect. One might recall the image used to advertise the Hollywood movie *The Day After Tomorrow*, 2004, depicting New York in the wake of climate change. This, after all, is an adventure movie. Furthermore, there is an argument that optimism is a valuable psychological state, because in common with other positive emotions, it acts to 'broaden individuals momentary thought-action repertoires, prompting them to pursue a wider range of thoughts and actions than is typical' (Fredrickson and Branigan 2005). Optimists in our previous study could have been focussing on the 'challenging' iconic images of climate change because they were interested in more divergent action against it. Some negative images may represent a challenge rather than just bad news in a way that images of skin cancer are unlikely to do.

Furthermore, iconic images of climate change are just one type of 'communication' about this global phenomenon, and we clearly need to recognise that despite their clear 'iconicity,' such images have complex psychological and emotional effects on us (Barthes 1957). One important question is how would level of dispositional optimism relate to attentional focus on more substantive climate change messages? And how might dispositional optimism affect so-called *optimism bias*, which has been reported frequently in the psychological literature and may be particularly relevant to climate change?

OPTIMISM BIAS

According to Tali Sharot (2011), around 80% of us suffer from some form of optimism bias in many aspects of our lives – apparently believing that our marriages will work ('it's only *other* marriages that fail,' we say), our start-up businesses will succeed and that we will have a long and fulfilling life compared to everyone else. This sort of unrealistic optimism would seem to be somewhat pervasive, affecting not only our personal relationships, but also our attitudes towards finance, work and health. For example, adolescent smokers are two-and-a-half times more likely than non-smokers to doubt that they personally will ever die from smoking, even if they smoked for 30 of 40 years; adult smokers are three times more likely to believe this. When it comes to smoking or climate change, this optimism bias can have deadly consequences.

Optimism bias has been found across a range of environmental issues (Gifford et al. 2009), as well as in estimates of the risk of health damage from specific environmental hazards, such as water pollution (Pahl et al. 2005), and with climate change (Gifford 2011). A large 18-nation survey demonstrated that individuals believe that across a number of environmental issues, they are safer than others living elsewhere in the world and that they are safer than future generations ever will be – in other words, they show both a spatial and a temporal bias.

Optimism bias appears to be associated with specific cognitive biases in processing relevant information. One study in behavioural neuroscience used Functional Magnetic Resonance Imaging (FMRI) to measure brain activity as participants estimated their probability of experiencing a range of negative life events, including things such as Alzheimer's and burglary (Sharot 2011). After each individual trial, participants were presented with the average probability of that event occurring to someone like him or herself. The researchers found that their participants were significantly more likely to change their estimate *only* if the new information was better than they had originally anticipated. This bias was reflected in their FMRI data in that optimism was related to a reduced level of neural coding of more negative than anticipated information about the future in the critical region of the frontal cortex (right inferior prefrontal gyrus). They also found that those participants highest in dispositional optimism were significantly worse at tracking this new *negative* information in this region, compared to those who were lower in dispositional optimism. In other words, the optimism bias derives partly from a failure to learn systematically from new undesirable information, and this bias was most pronounced with those highest in dispositional optimism.

Optimism may be highly advantageous for the individual, as Seligman has consistently argued, because it has significant effects on both mental and physical health (Seligman 2002) and was selected for during evolution (Mosing et al. 2009). Optimists live significantly longer and are much less likely to die from cardiac arrest (Scheier et al. 1989); optimism also increases the survival time after a diagnosis of cancer (Schulz 1996). It does this by reducing stress and anxiety about the future, and optimists consequently have better immune functioning (Segerstrom ct al. 1998). Belief in a positive future also encourages individuals (in *some* domains, particularly those that we have some control over) to behave in ways that can actually contribute to this positive future, thus becoming a self-fulfilling prophecy (Sharot 2011). Although underestimating future negative life events can reduce our stress levels and add to our longevity, sometimes, negative events really do need to be considered. Hence optimism bias can have very significant deleterious consequences, particularly regarding the discounting of serious risk.

Optimism bias is particularly relevant to issues concerning climate change. If we underestimate the probability of the negative effects of climate change happening to us, we may be much less likely to engage in mitigation behaviour, or sacrifice many of the things we currently value (foreign holidays, big cars and high carbon lifestyles) to reduce the risks associated with climate change. But how might we gain insight into cognitive biases in the area of climate change? We cannot present participants with the actual outcome data (as they did in the Sharot study) to see how they update their own estimates in the light of this because the catastrophic consequences of climate change are still largely in the future. However, could the research on biased patterns of attention provide us with any new insights here? After all, we are constantly being presented with articles documenting the scientific consensus on the likely effects of climate change, but could there be cognitive biases in how we attend to these messages? Does the evidence of differential focus on positive images by optimists in the Isaacowitz study have any relevance for how individuals attend to more serious substantive messages, as opposed to drawings and images?

VISUAL ATTENTION AND OPTIMISM

These considerations directed some new research by the authors into this phenomenon (Beattie et al. 2017). We used an eye tracker to record moment-to-moment individual gaze fixations as our participants read messages about climate change. On average, we read around 330 words per minute, and to achieve this large amount of information processing, we rapidly move our eyes forwards through the text between three to five times per second. Our eye movement behaviour largely consists of the actual eye movements (known as saccades) and periods in which the eyes do not move, but are relatively fixed in position. Research shows that very little information is processed during saccades and that instead it is during these gaze fixations that visual and cognitive processing takes place, such as word identification and semantic processing (in other words, the processing of meaning). The average fixation duration is approximately 200–250ms, but there are numerous factors that can influence fixation duration.

The massive research on eye movement behaviour (Rayner et al. 2012) suggests that although reading is largely a case of processing information word by word, there is more to reading than just identifying a word and moving on to the next word. Words need to be comprehended within their linguistic context, and the reader needs to extract the meaning out of successive sentences and parse these together to process the discourse of the text. To understand the discourse of the text may require the reader to draw on knowledge about the topic and to understand what the text is trying to convey. For example, the reader will need to establish what the text is trying to describe or suggest and judge whether they believe the claims that the text may make. This is an *active* process in which the reader's individual prior knowledge, their perspective on the situation, their moods, their attitudes and their intentions may influence how the message of the text is perceived and processed. Variations in overall fixation times and specific fixations may tell us a great deal about how people process messages and what specific aspects of the messages are being given the most attention.

In our study, we used a practice text and three articles about climate change – the first about climate change in general, the second about climate change and its relation to flooding in the United Kingdom and the third about climate change and its consequences for food scarcity and violent conflict. Each climate change article contained three arguments for climate change ('*for*') and three arguments against climate change ('*against*'). 'For' arguments were that climate change is real, human activity is the cause of both climate change generally and flooding in the UK, and predictions that climate change will cause both food scarcity and conflict. 'Against' arguments were that climate change is not occurring or is exaggerated, that it is not caused by human activity, that flooding in the United Kingdom is not caused by climate change and that there is no link between climate and either food scarcity or conflict. All arguments were drawn from print and electronic media (e.g. the *Guardian*, BBC News website) and online blogs. 'For' and 'against' arguments were edited such that they were of similar word count and frequency.

We also measured dispositional optimism using the ten-item Life Orientation Test, which is comprised of a series of simple statements such as 'In uncertain times, I usually expect the best.' A high score on this (e.g. 'I agree a lot') is taken to indicate a very high degree of optimism. We then split our participants into two groups based on their median score (optimists and non-optimists). The scan paths show individual fixations (represented by the circles) and the eye movements (the saccades) of two participants are shown next (see Figure 4.1a,b).

The text of the 'for' and 'against' arguments were grouped into Areas of Interest (AOI). Three dependent variables were used to assess attention: fixation count (number of individual eye-gaze fixations),

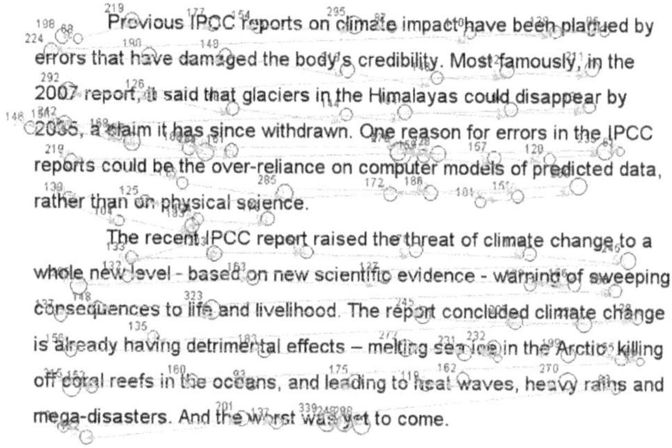

Previous IPCC reports on climate impact have been plagued by errors that have damaged the body's credibility. Most famously, in the 2007 report, it said that glaciers in the Himalayas could disappear by 2035, a claim it has since withdrawn. One reason for errors in the IPCC reports could be the over-reliance on computer models of predicted data, rather than on physical science.

The recent IPCC report raised the threat of climate change to a whole new level - based on new scientific evidence - warning of sweeping consequences to life and livelihood. The report concluded climate change is already having detrimental effects – melting sea ice in the Arctic, killing off coral reefs in the oceans, and leading to heat waves, heavy rains and mega-disasters. And the worst was yet to come.

a) Optimist

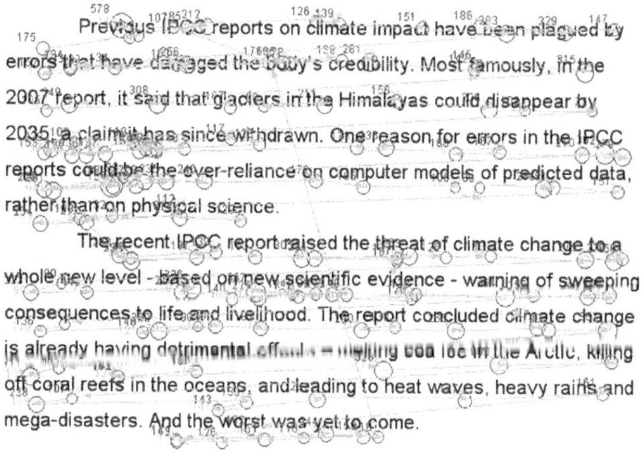

Previous IPCC reports on climate impact have been plagued by errors that have damaged the body's credibility. Most famously, in the 2007 report, it said that glaciers in the Himalayas could disappear by 2035, a claim it has since withdrawn. One reason for errors in the IPCC reports could be the over-reliance on computer models of predicted data, rather than on physical science.

The recent IPCC report raised the threat of climate change to a whole new level - based on new scientific evidence - warning of sweeping consequences to life and livelihood. The report concluded climate change is already having detrimental effects – melting sea ice in the Arctic, killing off coral reefs in the oceans, and leading to heat waves, heavy rains and mega-disasters. And the worst was yet to come.

b) Non-optimist

Figure 4.1 An individual scan path of a) an optimist and b) a non-optimist as they read arguments 'for' or 'against' climate change.

Note: Circles represent individual fixations on words, with larger circles representing longer fixation durations. Lines between circles represent saccadic eye-movement behaviour. In this example, the first paragraph is an argument against climate change, and the second paragraph is the argument for climate change.

average fixation duration and overall dwell time (total duration of all fixations within an AOI), which acts as an overall measure of reading time. We measured fixation count, fixation duration and dwell times to 'for' arguments and to 'against' arguments for both optimists and non-optimists (see Figure 4.2a,b).

The results of this study were very revealing. We found no significant relationship between level of dispositional optimism and the number of fixations to arguments either 'for' or 'against' climate change. However, there was a significant relationship between level of dispositional optimism and average fixation duration to 'for' arguments only. Optimism level was also significantly negatively correlated with average dwell time to both 'for' and 'against' arguments. Thus, higher levels of dispositional optimism are associated with less time spent attending to the content of the climate change articles irrespective of the particular argument (either 'for' or 'against') and shorter periods of time fixating on arguments 'for' climate change, as shown in Tables 4.1 and 4.2. In other words, optimists are turned off by *any* messages about climate change (either positive or negative), but they also spend less time fixating on messages arguing for climate change.

We were using eye tracking here as a measure of online processing of the messages about climate change, but how did this online processing affect what people remembered about the messages, given that in each article there were arguments both for and against? Do optimists (like Donald Trump – unfortunately not part of our study) who have shorter fixations on the arguments for climate change remember things differently?

We tested this by asking our participants to summarise the articles. We measured overall level of recall, which did not significantly differ, but we also analysed how each recalled article was framed. We employed three broad categories for coding how these recalled accounts were framed.

'For': the account was framed as being *primarily* about the evidence for climate change (and its general effects or specific effects on flooding, food scarcity and conflict, etc.) and the role of human activity in this.

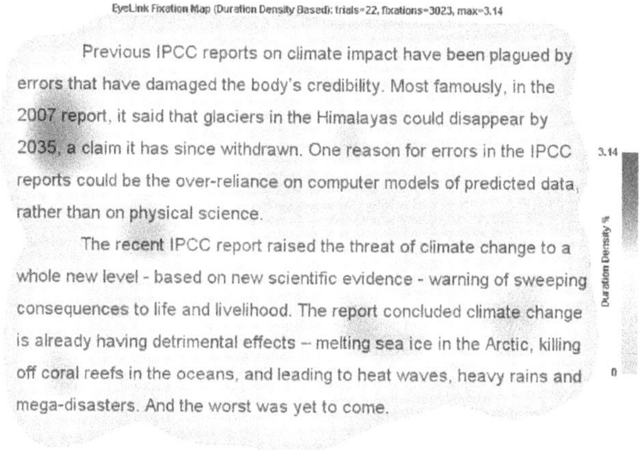

Previous IPCC reports on climate impact have been plagued by errors that have damaged the body's credibility. Most famously, in the 2007 report, it said that glaciers in the Himalayas could disappear by 2035, a claim it has since withdrawn. One reason for errors in the IPCC reports could be the over-reliance on computer models of predicted data, rather than on physical science.

The recent IPCC report raised the threat of climate change to a whole new level - based on new scientific evidence - warning of sweeping consequences to life and livelihood. The report concluded climate change is already having detrimental effects – melting sea ice in the Arctic, killing off coral reefs in the oceans, and leading to heat waves, heavy rains and mega-disasters. And the worst was yet to come.

a) Optimists

Previous IPCC reports on climate impact have been plagued by errors that have damaged the body's credibility. Most famously, in the 2007 report, it said that glaciers in the Himalayas could disappear by 2035, a claim it has since withdrawn. One reason for errors in the IPCC reports could be the over-reliance on computer models of predicted data, rather than on physical science.

The recent IPCC report raised the threat of climate change to a whole new level - based on new scientific evidence - warning of sweeping consequences to life and livelihood. The report concluded climate change is already having detrimental effects – melting sea ice in the Arctic, killing off coral reefs in the oceans, and leading to heat waves, heavy rains and mega-disasters. And the worst was yet to come.

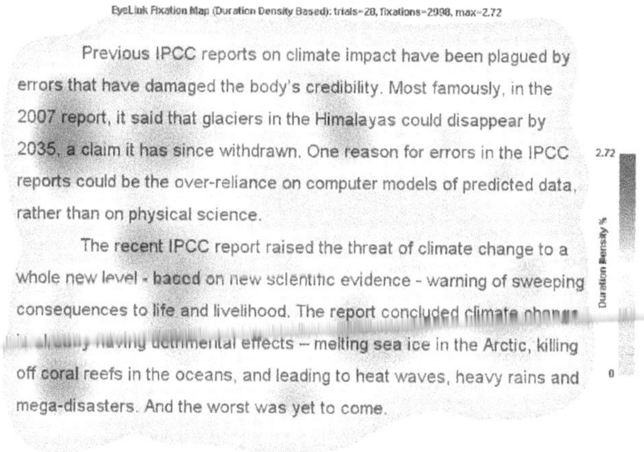

b) Non-optimists

Figure 4.2a,b A hotspot analysis of eye-gaze fixations of a group of optimists and non-optimists reading arguments 'for' or 'against' climate change.

Note: Greater intensity represents longer dwell times at fixated locations. In this example, the top paragraph in each case is an argument against climate change and the bottom paragraph in each case is the argument for climate change.

Table 4.1 Arguments **for** climate change

	Optimists Mean	Non-optimists Mean	Correlation Optimism Level/Gaze Measures
Fixation count	69.2	74.9	−0.220
Average fixation duration (milliseconds)	194.2	212.7	−0.327*
Overall dwell time (s)	13.3	15.9	−0.369*

Table 4.2 Arguments **against** climate change

	Optimists Mean	Non-optimists Mean	Correlation Optimism Level/Gaze Measures
Fixation count	67.7	74.2	−0.253
Average fixation duration (milliseconds)	198.2	211.7	−0.232
Overall dwell time (seconds)	13.3	15.9	−0.347*

'Against': the account was framed primarily in terms of there not really being a strong link between human activity and climate change (or its specific effects), or doubts about the very existence of climate change.

Debate: the account was framed as primarily being a debate between two opposing positions.

We found that non-optimists, who had longer fixations on the arguments 'for' climate change, were most likely to frame their recall in terms of the arguments for climate change ('this article is about global warming and how 95% of it is due to human activity'). Of their recalls, 66.7% were framed in this way. The optimists, on the other hand, who fixated significantly less on arguments 'for' climate change, were more likely to frame it in terms of a debate between two opposing positions ('it's about climate change, about trying to understand what's happening with the weather and there are different points of view'). Of their recalls, 66.7% were framed as a debate. There were few summaries of the content framed in terms of the arguments against climate change for either group (only 5% of the total).

Dispositional optimism thus seems to affect online processing of climate change messages and the framing of how these messages are recalled. We then decided to consider the relationship between level of dispositional optimism and the extent of optimism bias. With a new set of participants, we again measured level of dispositional optimism and devised a simple questionnaire to measure optimism bias. It consisted of three broad questions:

1 What is the probability of you personally being affected by climate change?
2 What proportion of people (living today) will be affected by climate change?
3 What proportion of future generations will be affected by climate change?

Participants had to write a number between 0% and 100% in response to each of the questions. Each of them had seven additional questions asking participants to rate (in the case of question 1) the probability of them being personally affected by severe drought/severe flooding/major threats to infrastructure/food shortages/major conflict/heat-related increased mortality and major disruption to their lives. In the case of the other questions, they had to rate the proportion of people living today being affected by each of these (question 2), and then the proportion of future generations being affected by them (question 3). There were thus 24 questions in all to assess possible optimism bias. We split our participants into three groups: 'optimists' (optimism score 18–23), 'medium-level optimists' (optimism score 15–17) and 'non-optimists' (optimism score 8–14).

We found that optimism bias is significantly affected by the underlying level of dispositional optimism – for example, *optimists* in our study reckoned that they had a 36.5% probability of being *personally* affected by climate change, whereas they thought that *other people* had a 52.8% probability of being affected by climate change and that 76.4% of future generations would be affected. For non-optimists, the figures were higher throughout − 56.8% thought that they would be personally affected, 68.5% thought that other people would be affected and 84.1% thought that future generations would be affected (see Table 4.3). Even non-optimists have some degree of optimism bias: they thought that they would be less likely to be personally affected by climate change than other people elsewhere and other people in the future. But the optimists in this sample were particularly blasé (they reckoned that they had about a one in three chance of personally being affected), which is perhaps worrying, given that there is a major self-help industry devoted to training people to be *even more optimistic*. However, sometimes a little *realism* about events and their causes in everyday life as a guide to future appropriate actions is very important.

Previous research had shown that optimism bias (overestimating the likelihood of positive events happening in our own life and underestimating the likelihood of negative events) derives partly from a failure to learn systematically from new undesirable information and that this bias is most pronounced with those highest in dispositional optimism. Other research has shown that dispositional optimists have an unconscious, automatic attentional bias to positive rather than negative stimuli. Our new research suggests that this attentional bias might also apply when individuals are presented with substantive messages about climate change. Many individuals are showing an attentional bias linked to maintaining their optimistic state when presented with climate change messages. Optimism may often have positive effects, because underestimating the likelihood of future negative events can reduce our levels of stress and anxiety about the future and add to our longevity. Many people, it seems, have developed cognitive strategies rooted in basic brain functioning that allows them to remain optimistic despite evidence to the contrary. The problem, however, is that some events really do need to be considered, and optimism bias can have very significant negative consequences, particularly regarding the discounting of serious risk. Climate change is one such risk.

Table 4.3 Mean estimates for participants varying in level of dispositional optimism for question 1

Question 1	Optimists	Medium-Level Optimists	Non-optimists
Q1.1: What is the probability of you personally being affected by climate change?	36.5	51.3	56.8
Q1.2: What is the probability of you personally being affected by severe drought because of climate change?	10.3	18.1	29.4
Q1.3: What is the probability of you personally being affected by severe flooding because of climate change?	18.2	22.6	38.8
Q1.4: What is the probability of you personally being affected by major threats to infrastructure because of climate change?	18.6	24.3	29.1
Q1.5: What is the probability of you personally being affected by food shortages because of climate change?	19.9	25.4	27.9
Q1.6: What is the probability of you personally being affected by major conflict over natural resources because of climate change?	19.8	31.8	35.4
Q1.7: What is the probability of you personally being affected by heat-related increased mortality because of climate change?	13.9	19.0	38.4
Q1.8: What is the probability of you personally suffering major disruption to your life because of climate change?	12.0	20.3	39.8

Of course, this research into cognitive biases, and particularly optimism bias, has a number of general implications. We cannot assume that members of the public are attending to messages about climate change in quite the same way (regardless of how credible the source is). The underlying messages may not be getting through because of an inherent cognitive bias designed to sustain emotional state and, of course, a very robust bias shaped by evolution. The research perhaps suggests that we should pay some regard to this bias in designing our communicational strategies about climate change. It may well not be enough simply to publicise the scientific evidence about climate change without framing it in a more optimistic way to highlight the positive aspects of mitigation strategies. A more positive overall frame about possible positive solutions should increase both feelings of self-efficacy and visual attention to the underlying message. Without this, we have the grave danger that many will selectively attend to the information and ultimately show little behavioural adaptation or indeed concern.

There is another important consideration here that is related to this. For the past few decades, we have been striving to increase optimism in society because of its health benefits (through both positive psychology and a cultural emphasis on 'the power of positive thinking'). Some have argued that we have produced a profound sociopsychological change, especially in Western societies with unrealistic expectations about the future (Ehrenreich 2010). They have also argued that it has actually 'undermined preparedness' to deal with real threats such as global terrorism, financial bubbles or climate change, with the public having 'no ability or inclination to imagine the worst.' Optimism can be a positive thing, but it has its limits. Over-optimism can be very damaging. Perhaps, it is time to reevaluate this overarching cultural focus and consider new ways to get the public to imagine the worse. However, this is unlikely to occur successfully on its own, unless we also spell out ways that can mitigate these effects.

This research should give us pause to think about climate change messages. We must remember the tendency for people to self-regulate their emotional state and the implications of this for how they attend to messages. We must also remember the implications of this selective processing for what they recall from these messages, how they frame it, and how they feel about the world. It's only human after all.

5

CLIMATE CHANGE CAMPAIGNS AND WHY THEY FAILED

We have already started considering what we must do about changing people's attitudes to climate change, and in this context, it is well worth considering what has been done so far to see what lessons can be learned. Our conclusion is that some climate change campaigns have gone very badly wrong. The goal of such campaigns should be to make us more aware of the issue of climate change, influence how we think about it, allow us to identify the role of human behaviour in contributing to it and critically change our behaviour in specific or in more general ways. Many of them fail to achieve any of these goals. Some just leave us a little puzzled.

WHY 9/11 IS NOT LIKE A TSUNAMI

Take, for example, the award-winning ad created by DDP for the World Wildlife Fund (WWF) in Brazil in 2009. Their campaign was designed to illustrate the devastating power of the Boxing Day tsunami which began as an earthquake off the northern tip of Sumatra on the morning of December 26, 2004. This tsunami devastated large areas of 14 countries, from Indonesia through to Tanzania and the Seychelles, killing over 280,000 people.

The WWF campaign was run on television, and it also appeared as a print advert. The theme of the ad was clear: associate 9/11 with the tsunami, using the process of classical conditioning, so that the less familiar tsunami would acquire some of the classically conditioned shock and fear response of the much more familiar 9/11. The intended goal was clearly to shock people out of their complacency. At the same time, by juxtaposing the two events, we can 'explain' the relative potency of the tsunami compared to 9/11 in terms of breadth of impact and number of lives lost.

Now, what, of course, is interesting about 9/11 (unlike many disasters) is that the majority of people have a very detailed 'flashbulb memory' about it, unlike many memories which are often quite sketchy. We can remember significant details of the images of 9/11 – the planes flying into the Twin Towers, and, in addition, we can recall considerable details of where we were and who we were with 17 years after the event. In many senses, this is extraordinary and suggests that our memories of events such as 9/11 are qualitatively different from our memories of most other events. Brown and Kulik (1977) coined the term 'flashbulb memory' to describe these sorts of memories. The majority of people tested in the United Kingdom also have flashbulb memories of the assassination of John F. Kennedy and Princess Diana's death in the crash in Paris. People can remember exactly where they were and what they were doing many years after these events (55 years in the case of the assassination of JFK). Brown and Kulik argued that flashbulb memories depend upon the joint action of two of the most primitive parts of the human brain: the reticular formation, which responds to surprise, and the limbic system, which responds to consequentiality. They argued that these memories are shaped by evolutionary pressures: the event is so significant that we encode details (including details of the situational context) in a particularly enduring way to guide our subsequent action (we will need to avoid these kinds of situations for our survival). One of the most interesting features of flashbulb memories is how selective our brains are in forming them (hardly a random firing of neurons). The two criteria that are usually cited are 'surprise' and 'consequentiality,' thus one of the authors (GB) has a flashbulb memory of hearing the news of his father's death as a 13-year-old boy (from his Uncle Terence in the wet car park of the Royal Victoria Hospital in Belfast). You can see immediately how this satisfies both criteria of surprise and consequentiality. But why does he have a flash-bulb memory for Princess Diana's death rather than say John Lennon's (Lennon and his music were of much more significance for his life than Princess Diana could ever have been)? Or perhaps even more puzzling, why does he have a flashbulb memory for Michael Jackson's death rather than David Bowie's, given that he was never a Michael Jackson fan but a *devotee* of Bowie? But given how selective these emotionally encoded memories are to specific events, how easy is it to transfer their effects using classical conditioning techniques based on the building of associative connections? And, in addition, given how detailed, far-reaching and *unconstrained* our flashbulb memories are of such events (with various features of the social and interpersonal context encoded in memory), are these really the best sources of data for what is a relative judgement task (i.e. the tsunami versus 9/11 in terms of impact)?

The WWF television advert begins with a high angle shot of the old iconic New York City skyline, complete with the Twin Towers of the World Trade Center. Just moments into the advert, we see the devastation of 9/11 unfold as the American Airline Flight 11 hits the North Tower of the World Trade Center between the 93rd and the 98th floor. Instantly, the thick black smoke begins to billow out of the tower. An image that shocked the world some 17 years ago – an image that is impossible to erase from our memories. The screen fades to black. Seconds later, we see the United Airlines Flight 175 crash into the South Tower of the World Trade Center. Again, we see the heavy smoke roar out of the North Tower, whilst the South Tower is embroiled in even thicker and blacker smoke. This wasn't something that happens in real life – this was something which you might expect to see in a disaster movie. Bold white text then appears on the screen: 'In 2001, one of the worst tragedies in the history of humanity killed 2,819 people.' The screen then cuts back to the Twin Towers. Still, thick black smoke is billowing out of each tower. We hear the faint sound of sirens and the screams of people who are running in every direction trying to escape the city. Dozens more aeroplanes then fly into the shot. The screen fades to black again. We see a flash of bold white text in the centre of the screen 'In 2005, the tsunami killed 280,000 people. That's 100 times more deaths. Our planet is brutally powerful. Respect it. Conserve it.'

The print advert had a similar theme. Again, we see an aerial shot with the familiar and iconic view of the New York City skyline. Take a closer look at the scene, and *dozens* of aeroplanes become visible – all aiming for the North or the South Tower of the World Trade Center. The words in the top right-hand corner, alongside the motif of the WWF panda read, 'The Tsunami killed 100 times more people than 9/11. The planet is brutally powerful. Respect it. Preserve it.'

The logic underpinning this campaign is somewhat shaky. The events of 9/11 were not foreseen nor anticipated (literally unfolding 'out of the clear blue sky,' as reflected in the title of the film by Daniel Gardner). Of course, the earthquake as the proximal stimulus for the tsunami was not foreseeable either – but climate change played a critical role in the development of the tsunami by raising sea levels in the area (see the interview with David King, the UK government's chief scientific adviser, in the *Guardian*, December 31, 2004). The effects of climate change on sea levels in certain parts of the world are possible to anticipate – this was part of the power of Al Gore's Nobel Prize-winning film *An Inconvenient Truth*. So it weakens the underlying conceptual message underpinning the WWF campaign by pairing a tsunami, that could be anticipated with something like 9/11, which could not. Events that cannot be anticipated, and we cannot avoid, just give rise to feelings of 'learned helplessness,' as the early research of Martin Seligman so persuasively demonstrated. The point of the campaign is to get us to take action against climate change, not to think that awful events happen without forewarning and without any possibility to take action, and that the tsunami is in essence like 9/11 and 'out of a clear blue sky.'

This campaign did cause a certain amount of outrage amongst those who saw it, not because of the kinds of reasons that we have just discussed which would affect its efficacy but because many argued that the WWF were exploiting 9/11. The WWF later apologised for this 'tasteless' and 'offensive' campaign (after firstly denying that it had ever been approved by the charity), and admitted that the adverts should never have been made. They blamed it on inexperienced staff who 'created and approved' them (so inexperienced that they even got the year wrong for the Asian tsunami). The magazine campaign subsequently won a merit award for public service at one of the most prestigious awards ceremonies in the US advertising industry. It was also submitted for an award at Cannes! What may work in terms of 'creativity,' however, might fall far short on conceptual, emotional and psychological grounds. This campaign failed because it did not consider the nature of associative processes, nor the constraints on them; it did not consider the formation and operation of human memory; it did not consider how emotion may transfer between stimuli (or fail to), and, perhaps most importantly of all, it did not consider why it is critical to leave the viewer with the feeling that he or she can actually do something to prevent similar events form occurring. If you don't leave people with a feeling of hope and the feeling that they can actually do something to prevent this – what is called self-efficacy, then you end up with either denial ('it will never occur') or a feeling of learned helplessness. Both, of course, are genuine disasters in this domain.

NURSERY RHYMES FOR ADULTS

In the United Kingdom, there have been a series of government campaigns with the intention of promoting pro-environmental behaviour by changing the public's perception of climate change. One such campaign was 'Act On CO_2,' launched in 2007. The campaign involved a series of magazine and television adverts to impact upon public awareness; these were designed to get people to reduce their carbon footprint through home energy use – e.g. switching off appliances, installing low energy light bulbs, fitting the correct amount and type of home insulation. These early adverts aimed to encourage individuals to do their bit by tying in pro-environmental behaviour with saving money. For example, one particular advert included the caption, 'Simple actions reduce both fuel bills and CO_2 emissions. Making your home as energy efficient as possible could save you over three hundred pounds a year. Save money, save energy.'

In 2010, Act On CO_2 launched their 'Bedtime Story' ad. The ad portrays a father reading a bedtime story to his young daughter about the seriousness of climate change, emphasising the implications and consequences of climate change for the next generation. The father reads aloud about 'awful heatwaves,' 'terrible storms and floods' and the devastating effects CO_2 is having on the planet – all because the adults used energy. The audience sees animated sketches of rabbits crying, drawings of people floating on beds in flooding waters and a drowning cat balancing on an upturned table clinging on for dear life. The daughter then asks if there is going to be a happy ending to the story. The advert ends with a voiceover telling the audience, 'It is up to us how the story ends' emphasising that the future of the planet is now down to the viewer (hopefully now feeling very guilty).

The driver here is obvious. It's guilt. The father has to justify his actions or lack of action to his daughter in a familiar context: the bedtime story. But the problem is that many things happen in classic bedtime stories that could never happen in real life. Consider fairy tales, for example, the archetypal bedtime story, with the big bad wolf dressed as a grandmother. Fairy tales cannot happen; that's the point of them. They are made up (and retold across generations) for the purpose of stimulating children's imaginations and teaching them some important lessons – in this particular case to be wary of strangers and not to rely on first impressions (indeed *Little Red Riding Hood* has been interpreted to act as a moral tale based around this concept). Everything dressed as a grandmother is not a grandmother; that's the lesson here: don't be fooled by strangers. Adults, of course, understand the semiotics of these stories. They know that they are far-fetched, *impossible* accounts of the imagination, critically requiring the imagination of a child to make them engaging. Of course, there can be no real consequences for the protagonists in these stories ('no wolf was harmed in the making of this production'). The only conceivable consequence is the fear response in the child hearing the story. And so back to the ad, we have an interpretative frame for bedtime stories (improbable events, heavy moral undertones, no possible real consequences for any of those involved) that has not really been considered by those who devised the campaign. And, as before, there are no specific actions prescribed. The campaign didn't offer any specific guidance to the audience in order for them to break down the barriers to allow them to adopt a new low carbon lifestyle, and there was no attempt to persuade them that these behaviours could make a difference. Therefore, it makes no attempt to increase the feelings of self-efficacy in the viewer and ignores altogether consideration of response efficacy (inculcating the belief that the behaviour advocated will actually make a difference to the proposed threat).

The campaign relied heavily on guilt and fear of a possible future to promote behaviour change. Using fear in a campaign can work, as long as there are clear action steps presented to the audience for them to negate the threat. However, if the level of fear in a campaign is high, and there are no clear action steps to negate the threat, the level of self-efficacy will be low, and the audience will more likely to reject the message, resulting in denial or severe criticism of both the message and the messenger ('patronising,' 'over-simplistic,' 'guilt trip,' 'condescending').

Another magazine campaign, again commissioned by 'Act on CO_2,' parodied certain nursery rhymes, illustrating them with doomed images to portray the negative effects of climate change. One particular ad showed sketches of three men in a bathtub floating in water surrounded by houses and cars which were partially submerged under the water with the words 'rub a dub dub, three men in a tub, a necessary course of action due to flash flooding caused by climate change.' The text then continued,

> Climate change is happening. Temperatures and sea levels are rising. Extreme weather events such as storms, floods and heatwaves will become more frequent and intense. If we carry on at this rate, life in 25 years could be very different.

A second magazine ad used a drawing to portray a young boy and girl at the top of a hill looking down a water well searching for water, which was not there, with the words 'Jack and Jill could not fetch a pail of water because extreme weather due to climate change had caused a drought.' Both ads warned that 'it's our children who'll really pay the price of climate change.' But again, these print ads were extremely negative, and there was little emphasis on ways to solve the problem. In addition, the sketched images of Jack and Jill on an impossible mission trying to collect water from a dried up well (a children's story again), or the drawings of the three men looking helpless, floating in a bathtub in a street flooded with water surrounded by submerged houses and cars did little by way of connecting with the audience (with the text from the classic nursery rhyme which dates back to the 14th century, a nursery rhyme with a somewhat lascivious origin – it was originally three *maids* in the tub, where the 'tub' was a fairground attraction similar to a modern peep show). These have all of the problems of the bedtime story frame; we are not being primed (i.e. unconsciously influenced) to think of *our children* so much as being primed to think of this particular genre of communication (bedtime story, nursery rhyme) aimed at children, too immature and inexperienced to react more critically to them. And, again, they are all very negative.

Perhaps focussing on the positive aspects of sustainable behaviour – the long bike rides along the idyllic country roads in the spring, the family picnics in the roving hills on a glorious summer's day would have more success. Or perhaps by presenting the audience with examples of positive outcomes of engaging in pro-environmental behaviour, rather than presenting negative consequences of not engaging in pro-environmental behaviour, will inspire people to start making the small changes that are necessary.

WHEN DOES FEAR WORK?

So why are fear and shock tactics appropriate for some campaigns and not for others? They clearly have been used successfully in some campaigns in other domains, including smoking. For example, in 2004, a £4m anti-smoking campaign was launched across the United Kingdom using various advertising mediums. The campaign used strong imagery depicting fat oozing out of a smoker's artery. This was one of the British Heart Foundation's most successful campaigns to date. The adverts, showed a cigarette which was used to represent a smoker's artery with the words 'give up before you clog up.' This appeared in magazines, newspapers, on television and on billboards across the country in a bid to make smokers aware of the danger of cigarettes. In the first month of the campaign, a total of 10,000 people called the charity's smoking health line, and a further 62,000 visited its website in search of tips to give up smoking and a total of 14,000 people gave up smoking as a result of this (highly memorable) campaign. The Department of Health brought out another hard-hitting, anti-smoking shock campaign in 2012. This time the campaign used dramatic imagery of tumours growing on cigarettes as they were being smoked. The message behind this campaign was that 'every 15 cigarettes you smoke cause a mutation that can become cancer.' This campaign helped reduce smoking rates in the United Kingdom to their lowest level of 18.4% (Department of Health 2014).

The Act on CO_2 campaign and the British Heart Foundation's quit smoking campaign were (superficially) quite similar in many ways. They both included some basic information – in one case about the devastating effects of CO_2 on the earth's atmosphere, in the other about the health risks that cigarettes cause to the individual smoker. They both focussed on the negative consequences of behaviour, but a very different sort of imagery was used in the two cases, and this may be critical. One used sketches (from children's stories or nursery rhymes) to depict the consequences of climate change (drowning rabbits, a bath floating in water, Jack and Jill not able to collect water from the well). The other represented the effects that cigarettes have on smoker's health (with fat oozing from the cigarettes as they are being smoked to represent a smoker's clogged up artery in the 2004 ad, or the cancerous tumours growing on cigarettes in the 2012 ad). You can see from our research on optimism bias and eye tracking outlined in the last chapter why this might be very effective. If you depict a real artery sliced open to reveal fat, or a cancerous tumour on a body, you might well find an automatic and immediate aversion of gaze to maintain (some degree of) emotional equilibrium. Cigarettes oozing fat, or cancerous tumours in a cigarette, however, are novel stimuli that draw our attention, particularly because at first you cannot work out what is happening. On the other hand, drawings suitable for children are unlikely to attract the gaze of adults.

Both campaigns also publicised websites that the viewers could go to if they wanted more information. But the smoking ad has a clear message: 'You have to stop smoking' (with a declared, and empathetic, recognition that this is not going to be easy, but that it's the 'smart' thing to do); the climate change message was incredibly vague in terms of recommended action. 'See what you can do,' the melodious voiceover says at the end, as if the makers of the ad weren't sure themselves ('answers on a postcard, please'). The Act on CO_2 ad also reinforces the temporal bias in the adult viewer, saying explicitly, 'It was the children of the [imaginary] land who'd have to live with the horrible consequences.' In other words, climate change is something for the future and not of immediate concern for adults at least. One campaign highlights the effects on the individual, the other highlights in schematic form the possible effects on future generations. One is a call to action; the other is not.

The imagery in these sorts of ads is, of course critical, and many campaigns have got this wrong. Wang and her colleagues (2017) have argued that there are far too many polar bears and melting ice caps in climate change campaigns. Indeed, the polar bear has become the somewhat clichéd iconic image of climate change and was even represented on the Coca Cola can in 2011 to show that they cared about sustainability (a somewhat mixed message if ever there was one for a sugary product in an aluminium non-biodegradable can). Wang points out that the images used rarely, if at all, show the effect that climate change is having on human beings, and when humans are used in climate change campaigns, they are usually from countries in distant parts of the world – parts of the world that are very different to our own (thus increasing the spatial bias). Or they use politicians trying to get the messages across. Perhaps if messages regarding climate change included the risk to the health and well-being of the recipient of the message, then they might be more effective.

SO WHAT WOULD A SUCCESSFUL CAMPAIGN LOOK LIKE?

So how can we create a successful campaign to engage the audience and bring about a positive change in behaviour? In 2008, the National Endowment for Science, Technology and the Arts (NESTA) issued a report which represented a very useful appraisal of the extent of this problem and evaluated a range of possible solutions. They reviewed various initiatives and concluded that there was very little evidence of behaviour change to date to reduce emissions – quite the opposite in fact. Between 1990 and 2005, they say that household energy rose by 40%, and between 2005 and 2006, CO_2 emissions from international aviation rose by 1.5%. CO_2 from transport rose 1.3% in 2006 over the previous year. Our criticism of these campaigns in the preceding pages might well have been justified.

They offer a number of insights. It's important to identify climate change as a common enemy which can draw people together. We need to focus on effective immediate actions that people can take to stop them feeling overwhelmed by the seriousness and the scale of the problem. Another key insight is that we should avoid guilt as a motivator by not implying that people's everyday behaviour is to blame for the problem. The problem with campaigns that use negative emotion, such as guilt and fear and anxiety, is that if people don't feel that they can do anything immediately to help solve the problem (low self-efficacy), then they typically find other ways of dealing with the threat as Witte and Allen have pointed out (2000), and we have discussed. These include defensive avoidance ('too scary, don't think about it'), denial ('this won't happen to me') and reactance ('they're just trying to manipulate me'). Reactance was probably the way that many viewers dismissed the 'Act on CO_2' bedtime story ads. After all, if bedtime stories are moral tales to manipulate children, then they are likely to be perceived in these ads as an attempt to manipulate adults. Other key insights are that if one is trying to promote a less consumption-intensive lifestyle, then this can be presented as an *opportunity* to spend more time with friends and family rather than as an issue of self-sacrifice and deprivation. They also recognise that campaigns can be aimed at people and not only as individuals, but also as members of various groups and communities (including familial, neighbourhood, work groups, etc.), and that the campaign may want to bolster feelings of community, solidarity and identity to encourage activities such as car share or community recycling. Another key insight from social marketing is to strategically focus any campaigns in terms of target behaviours, by focussing on consumption linked to those products with the most significant effects on climate change. They cite the work of the European Environmental Impact of Products from 2005, which assessed the environmental effect of 255 environmental products and found that 70% to 80% of the total impact derived from food and drink consumption, housing (including domestic energy) and transport (including commuting, leisure and community travel). DEFRA subsequently took some of these considerations on board.

The NESTA report suggests a number of ways forward for climate change campaigns, including promoting more sustainable behaviours as the 'normal' and 'sensible' thing to do, avoiding being too 'miserable' about the consequences of not acting, about fairness (the public will do their bit if governments will lead by example) and that climate change is personally relevant – that is to say, the risks are not just going to be faced by distant countries or future generations. The report says, 'Recent campaigns have struggled to change behaviour because they have neglected the importance of opportunities and the power of positive emotions in responding to climate change.' (2008: 43). We have already seen a number of campaigns based on negative emotion; instead, we need to focus on the positive benefits for more sustainable behaviours. We need to tell people what they can do specifically (turning off appliances when not in use, driving more smoothly to use less fuel, using reusable cups, choosing low carbon alternatives). But we need to persuade them that these actions are going to be replicated by other members of their family and by many others in their neighbourhood, country and city, and therefore, it will make a difference – that everyone is going to do their bit. In addition, we need to remind people that there are enormous opportunities (including emotional benefits) to be had from engaging in other low carbon lifestyles. You can leave your car at home when you go to the shop and walk instead, and feel healthier and fitter and lose weight; you can work from home more and save fuel and see more of your family; you can become an environmental champion as part of your overall identity – impressive when introducing yourself to a stranger (if perhaps a little cheesy).

What is most interesting about the NESTA report is that it follows the logic of Melinda Gates and others that we can learn important lessons from the hard commercial world that sold us so much stuff that we didn't need and gave us so many bad habits. The commercial world and the big tobacco companies managed to get the world to smoke, so can we use their techniques to get the world to do positive things regarding our planet? Some of the campaigns that we reviewed at the start of this chapter, in our view, were never going to work – there were too many conceptual and practical flaws within them. They had little effect because they failed to connect with our rational brain or with our emotional brain. They were low on memorability. We had to keep returning to the Act On CO_2 ad to try to remember the story that the child was being told (and was a 5-year-old child really meant to understand the concept of CO_2 that was mentioned several times?). The relationship between rational and emotional processing of the message were not well thought out, nor planned. Remedial actions were not specified and were vague in the extreme. The temporal bias, explicit in the Act On CO_2 ad, minimised personal relevance. We need new ideas.

6

HARD LESSONS FROM CIGARETTE ADVERTISING

Of course, we may have to be creative when it comes to climate change, perhaps extremely creative, to take Melinda Gates seriously. How radical can we be? Why not consider how the big tobacco companies got the world hooked on smoking? That radical? When it was still legal, cigarette advertising was an enormous success. In 1965, 51.1% of American men smoked, and 33.3% of American women, and it was already well established at that time that smoking was associated with cancer. So what did the tobacco companies know that we don't?

In a recent book, one of authors discussed the role of Ernest Dichter, a psychoanalyst, in this enterprise (Beattie 2018). Psychoanalysis was providing new insights into how the mind works; the emerging metaphor was that the human mind is like a glacier, most of it is hidden from view. Human beings may be rational creatures, but not rational all of the time, and there are unconscious forces that govern much of our lives. This might have been a popular notion in psychoanalysis at that time (indeed a central notion), but not in academic psychology. Kahneman's contemporary theorising about the role of the unconscious 'System 1' in everyday cognition might well be changing that now. Could marketing tap into these unconscious forces? Dichter decided to turn his attention away from the curing of neuroses using psychoanalytic methods to the application of psychoanalytic understanding of marketing. There were more similarities than differences between the two enterprises, he thought. People say that they are not subject to neurotic complexes, and people say that they are not open to manipulation through advertising. However, people say many things; the reality might be quite different. Both enterprises need a clear model of the mind. You need to see below the surface, to *access* the unconscious to cure neurosis and to *manipulate* the unconscious to sell brands. If you want to understand how people think and feel about products, you cannot just ask them directly. Psychoanalysts would never do that; it would be ludicrous ('please tell me about your neurosis'); you need more indirect and more intense methods. You need the psychoanalyst's couch, but on an industrial scale.

Dichter developed a completely new *approach* to uncover the more irrational and unconscious side of consumer behaviour. He said that we need to start at the very beginning, indeed with our first point of contact with the consumer. Interviews can be revealing for market research, he argued, but these interviews need to change fundamentally. He suggested that much smaller numbers of respondents should be interviewed (after all, many of the great insights of psychoanalysis were based on single case studies). But these interviews needed to be much longer and much more in-depth, on the assumption that if you let people talk long enough, you may be able to find something interesting in the associations between concepts that come tumbling out in spontaneous speech often in unguarded moments when the ego is less in control. You also need to get respondents to talk indirectly (rather than directly) about the product. You need to get them to verbalise their feelings; you need to listen carefully; you need to check and crosscheck, and you need to listen for inconsistencies. You do not take what they say at face value; you need to understand instead the symbolic importance of products in people's lives, and you need to interpret what they say.

One of his core principles was 'the principle of fundamental insights.' He says that the point about human motivation is that we, as actors, have no real idea why we do one thing rather than another.

> In practising research on human motivations, we feel it to be our duty to get down to fundamental insights, to accept the fact without fear or embarrassment that quite a number of human motivations are irrational, unconscious, unknown to the people themselves. This principle means that most human actions have deeper motivations than those which appear on the surface, motivations which can be uncovered if the right approach is used.
>
> (Dichter 1960: 45)

Of course, if you ask people why they do something, they will give you an answer ('we are not allowed by our culture to admit true irrationality as an explanation of our behaviour'), so he avoided asking them. Instead, he allowed them to talk indirectly and in-depth ('tell me about your first cigarette'). He encouraged them to disclose their emotions and to talk about the extremes ('tell me about the best beer you ever had and the worst beer you ever had'). The reasoning here was to mobilise 'true feelings' and 'real experience,' and to move away from 'considered opinions.' He encouraged them to be specific. When people talk in terms of generalities it is easier for them to present a 'rational' and considered view of things. However, perhaps most importantly of all, he encouraged them to be spontaneous, and then he analysed them carefully to work out their true feelings and intentions. In other words, this was an approach that did not take what people said at face value. He filmed his respondents interacting with various products (women were often surprised by how much time they spent sliding their fingers over a bar of soap to test its smoothness). He used psychodrama where they acted out their relationship with the product (the sound of the fist on the glove is a crucial dimension for baseball gloves). He used various projective techniques ('imagine that you are a little boy looking though a keyhole into a kitchen ten years from now. What do you see?').

His first major professional success was with the Compton Advertising Agency to promote Ivory soap, whose sales had significantly slumped at that time. 'The soap that floats' had been discovered by accident in 1879; it had been performing extremely well for many years. The standard market research approach had been to ask consumers why they chose this particular product, or why they didn't. Dichter wanted to apply his 'functional principle.' He said that there was no point in trying to promote a brand of soap before you understood more about the psychology of bathing, so he began by interviewing 100 people at various YMCA's around the country in his usual non-directive way. 'I decided to talk to people about such things as daily baths and showers, rather than to ask people various questions about why they used or did not use Ivory Soap' (Dichter 1960: 33). Bathing, he discovered, had all kinds of hidden psychological significance. It was not just to do with washing dirt away for some people; rather, it was a process of psychological cleansing as well. As he himself put it, 'You cleanse yourself not only of dirt but of guilt.' The slogan that he came up with was 'Be smart and get a fresh start with Ivory soap. . . . and wash all your troubles away.' Sales of Ivory soap shot up. By 1979, according to *Advertising Age*, Ivory had sold more than 30 billion bars.

Soon enough, he turned to smoking. His starting assumption was that cigarette advertising up to that point had got it seriously wrong. The ads at that time were all designed to emphasise the flavour of the cigarette, or how mild they were (the Chesterfield ad from the 1940s had Alan Ladd say, 'I like Chesterfields – they're my brand because they're MILD'; 'Lucky Strikes means Fine Tobacco'). Based on depth interviews with 350 smokers, Dichter concluded that things such as taste, mildness or flavour were 'minor considerations' when it comes to smoking; the main appeal of cigarettes was the range of psychological pleasures that you get from them. He argued that, from a psychological point of view, cigarettes work in a number of distinct ways. Firstly, they allow you to behave like a child again, able to 'follow your whims.' They offer a 'legitimate excuse for interrupting work and snatching a moment of pleasure.' Like children, we crave rewards – 'a cigarette is a reward that we can give ourselves as often as we wish.' Dichter argued that they should use this insight of self-reward as the basis for a marketing campaign.

However, that was only part of his observations about the nature of smoking as an *activity*. Some of his respondents had also commented that with cigarettes, you never really feel alone. Perhaps, this was tapping into the primitive concept of fire, a warm glow, a conditioned stimulus rooted in our evolutionary past associated with the group assembling around the fire. One of Dichter's respondents said 'when I see the glow in the dark, I am not alone any more,' and Dichter added that the use of cigarettes to combat feelings of loneliness and isolation was critical. He also added that 'the companionable character of cigarettes is also reflected in the fact that they help us make friends.' This insight formed the basis of a number of marketing campaigns.

The emphasis in his approach was on understanding the range of roles and functions that cigarettes can play in people's lives. In other words, he wanted to start with some psychological understanding of what cigarettes *do* in people's lives, following again what he had learned from his reading of Margaret Mead and other cultural anthropologists. His functional analysis built from there. Repeatedly, he found that people smoke to relieve tension and as a reward for something that they have done. They smoke to reduce stress in anticipation of an event. They smoke as a symbolic statement about how daring they are. They smoke as a way of bonding with others. They smoke as part of a ritualised performance that requires little planning, but it allows for a projection of sophistication. Cigarettes are used before sex because people are nervous, and after sex as a relaxing reward. All of these observations are critical in the marketing process.

Then, of course, there is the oral pleasure that derives from smoking, 'as fundamental as sexuality and hunger.' Here he was reminded of some great psychoanalytic truths about early stages of psychological development and frustration and how people deal with it. What is smoking in essence? It is a form of behaviour, heavily over-laden with symbolic and social connotations, where you put something in your lips to comfort yourself at times of stress or frustration, or as a reward. It is about oral gratification, as infantile (in the context of Freudian theory) as sucking your thumb. However, it is a socially acceptable way of obtaining this oral gratification by simultaneously sending out a powerful message about virile maturity and potency. It is so powerful because it simultaneously satisfies infantile desires and yet symbolically sends out a very adult signal. Dichter also highlighted the power of lighting a cigarette (as well, of course, as its more 'social' connotations). It was the power of fire that helped define and shape homo sapiens in evolutionary terms.

Dichter says that we have to recognise the psychological needs associated with smoking and what smoking provides us within our everyday lives. At the same time, Dichter argued that we have to deal with the essential psychological conflict that smoking generates. He wrote, 'One of the main jobs of the advertiser in this conflict between pleasure and guilt is not so much to sell the product as to give moral permission to have fun without guilt.' The guilt associated with smoking was compounded by the fact that by the 1950s there was growing evidence that smoking was indeed very harmful (although Dichter is cynically dismissive of the accumulating evidence – 'Scientific and medical studies on the physiological effects of smoking provide a confused picture: Some conclude that smoking is harmful; others deny it. This same confusion prevails among smokers them-selves'). Cigarette companies were trying to use the message that they would not kill you as part of their pitch. This was often done by having doctors (and dentists interestingly enough) recommend particular brands as being 'healthier.' Dichter thought that this was fundamentally misguided. It was unconsciously associating cigarette smoking with increased mortality, the 'not' was not necessarily the critical element in how such messages were interpreted by the public. Dichter concluded that smoking offers 'a psychological satisfaction sufficient to overcome health fears, to withstand moral censure, ridi-cule, or even the paradoxical weakness of "enslavement to habit."' Ads now focussed on powerful men relaxing with a cigarette as a reward for their efforts. Sometimes, these busy, powerful men with their feet up were doctors. However, this was not a doctor trying to reassure you that the cigarettes would not kill you; this was 'one of the busiest men in town . . . on call 24 hours a day . . . a scientist, a diplomat, and a friendly sympathetic human being all in one,' taking a hard-earned rest and smoking for pleasure. These ads had everything; they broke the associative connection between smoking and health/ill health/mortality/death highlighted in the previous ads involving doctors by using the doctor merely as a reassuring role model and an exemplar of the class of busy, successful men who deserve a break. In addition, the doctor is described as a 'scientist' no less. A scientist who was presumably capable of evaluating the accumulating evidence and then making a conscious, reflective choice to smoke Camels ('More Doctors smoke Camels than any other cigarette'). Interestingly, the capital 'M' in 'More' and the capital 'D' in 'Doctors' are in red (thus 'M.D.'), to use a perceptual grouping cue, to pull the letters 'M' and 'D' together and to make them stand out from their background. In other words, we are talking here about medical doctors – real doctors. These were powerful and effective ads in terms of their effects – that is to say, their sales figures.

However, Dichter did something else in his work on the psychology of smoking and the effective marketing of cigarettes that has rarely been commented on. He laid down a marker for future attempts to defend smoking and the promotion of smoking by suggesting that any evidence for a statistical relationship between smoking and ill health could very well be an artefact of something else. He wrote:

> Efforts to reduce the amount of smoking signify a willingness to sacrifice pleasure in order to assuage . . . feelings of guilt. The mind has a powerful influence on the body, and may produce symptoms of physical illness. Guilt feelings may cause harmful physical effects not at all caused by the cigarettes used, which may be extremely mild. Such guilt feelings alone may be the real cause of the injurious consequences.

> (Dichter 1960)

In other words, it is not smoking that gives you the cancer; it is the guilt that you have about smoking (and this guilt originally derives from your parents attempting to censure this form of behaviour in their offspring, even when they themselves smoked). Don't blame cigarettes for your ill health; blame your parents! However, bear in mind that he had also said that the role of the advertiser was 'not so much to sell the product as to give moral permission to have fun without guilt.' He was going to help us have fun without guilt and, therefore, reduce the physical harm of smoking.

In 2011, Pettigrew and Lee carried out an extensive review of recently released tobacco industry documents (released because of litigation) that revealed a great deal about how the industry fought back against the growing scientific evidence on the relationship between smoking and lung cancer. The tobacco industry wanted to open up a great 'debate' about the effects of smoking on health, to suggest that the medical evidence was far from conclusive and to show that there were differences of opinion amongst experts on this topic. The tobacco industry created the Council for Tobacco Research in 1953 to fund research that could be used in this fight. One recipient of this funding was the distinguished scientist Hans Selye, the so-called father of stress, who had extremely impressive academic credentials with 1,700 articles and 39 books to his name (and nominated for the Nobel Prize 10 times). Pettigrew and Lee discovered that it was Selye who first contacted the tobacco industry as far back as 1958, seeking funding for his research on stress. This first request was not successful. However, the following year, a law firm representing the tobacco industry now involved in litigation, wrote to Selye offering him US $1,000 to write a memorandum demonstrating that 'medicine has previously seen striking correlations suggested as representing cause and effect, only later to find that the significance, if any, of the correlation was otherwise' (Pettigrew and Lee 2011: 412). Selye agreed to do this for the money offered, but only on the understanding that any quotes used would not be attributed to him; neither did he want to appear as a witness in any court case. This, as they say, was just the start of a very long and rewarding relationship. Given his academic credentials, he was of enormous value to them. He was, after all, an objective scientist, or at least that's how it would have seemed to the public if they did not know about his financial connection with the industry. Selye advised the tobacco industry that it should defend itself by focussing on the 'prophylactic and curative' aspect of smoking. Smoking was to be marketed as a way of adjusting to a stressful lifestyle. Selye was prepared to argue that it is stress that kills rather than smoking. Smoking, he suggested, can actually help you cope with this stress; it was in fact beneficial. In 1969, Selye, according to Pettigrew and Lee, 'testified before the Canadian House of Commons Health Committee arguing against anti-smoking legislation, opposing advertising restrictions, health warnings, and restrictions on tar and nicotine' (2011: 413). He was being funded to the tune of US $100,000 a year back in the 1960s (about three-quarters of a million dollars in today's money). He appeared on the Canadian Broadcasting Corporation, arguing for the benefits of smoking for those under stress. Smoking, he argued, was a 'diversion' to avoid disease-causing stress. Oddly, he failed to mention this conflict of interest in the broadcast; he failed to point out that the tobacco industry was paying him as a spokesperson.

In the United Kingdom, in the meantime, Hans Eysenck was playing a similar role in this 'debate' about the harmful effects of smoking. He was another very high-profile and influential academic who publicly disputed the link between smoking and health. Like Selye, he was also secretly receiving money from the tobacco industry, from the 1960s onwards. Eysenck's hypothesis was that there are certain types of personality who are prone to cancer and that there are certain types of personality inclined to smoke (Eysenck 1966). He argued that it was personality that was the critical and confounded factor in cancer risk (Dichter, of course, had said that it was 'guilt' that was the confounded factor. Selye said it was 'stress'; clearly money bought a lot of possible unaccounted for factors). Eysenck proposed that certain types of personality – namely, extroverts – are drawn to nicotine because it is a stimulant and therefore has introverting effects; in other words, extraverts smoke for good 'genetically determined' reasons.

We now know that Eysenck received more than £800,000 through a secret US tobacco fund called Special Account Number 4 (*The Independent*, October 31, 1996). Eysenck was, of course, not alone in secretly taking this money, as we have already seen.

MERCHANTS OF DOUBT

Oreskes and Conway, in their book *Merchants of Doubt*, describe how on December 15, 1953, the presidents of four of America's largest tobacco companies, American Tobacco, Benson and Hedges, Philip Morris and US Tobacco, met with John Hill, the CEO of the public relations firm Hill and Knowlton, at the Plaza Hotel in New York. Their aim was to challenge the scientific evidence that smoking could kill you. In the words of the authors,

> They would work together to convince the public that there was 'no sound scientific basis for the charges,' and that the recent reports [about cigarette tar and cancer] were simply 'sensational accusations' made by publicity-seeking scientists hoping to attract more funds for their research. They would not sit idly by while their product was vilified; instead, they would create a Tobacco Industry Committee for Public Information to supply a 'positive' and 'entirely pro-cigarette' message to counter the anti-cigarette one. As the US Department of Justice would later put it, they decided, 'to deceive the American public about the health effects of smoking'. At first, the companies did not think they needed to fund new scientific research, thinking it would be sufficient to 'disseminate information on hand.' John Hill disagreed, 'emphatically warn[ing] . . . . that they should . . . sponsor additional research,' and that this would be a long-term project. He also suggested including the word 'research' in the title of their new committee, because a pro-cigarette message would need science to back it up. At the end of the day, Hill concluded, 'scientific doubts must remain.'

Eysenck is not mentioned in the book on those who marketed doubt for a living. But his work, along with Selye and many others, contributed greatly to the uncertainty about smoking and cancer, and again in the words of Oreskes and Conway, 'throughout the 1950s and well into the 1960s, newspapers and magazines presented the smoking issue as a great debate rather than as a scientific problem in which evidence was rapidly accumulating.' Oreskes and Conway also point out striking parallels with how the scientific 'debate' about climate change was similarly manufactured, with right-wing attacks co-ordinated by right-wing organisations and media on the 'watermelons' – green on the outside, red on the inside. These right-wing organisations feared the regulation of the free market demanded by environmentalists as the slippery slope to Communism. The rest of the media, keen to be seen as fair and balanced, liked to provide both sides of the argument, so the pro-lobby and the anti-lobby were (and are) both afforded the opportunities to promote their argument, and the recipients of all of these media messages then tune in and tune out as we have seen in Chapter 4, sometimes with devastating effect.

Smoking is a great moral tale for climate change with so many important similarities at all sorts of levels, and yet because Dichter's thinking preceded that of Zajonc, Slovic and Kahneman (with their eventual recognition that human beings are not rational in their decision making, although people may well have to rationalise and justify their actions), we may learn a great deal from the campaigns that drove smoking forward. Dichter argued that asking people why they do things does not really work. Too much of our mental life operates without conscious awareness. We need to target unconscious motivations and allow these new emotional associations linked to these underlying motivations to drive our decision making. But at the same time to set up a 'debate' so that the fair media, always wanting to represent both sides of an argument, give people something to use when they have to explain why they are still smoking or living a very high carbon lifestyle to others. However, at a deeper level, smoking had it easy in that it was easier to identify what psychological needs smoking could satisfy (self-comforting, self-reward, bonding with others etc.). With climate change, we have to unpick the deep psychological desires that high carbon lifestyles satisfy and then think how we can make their low carbon counterparts equally desirable so that they too can become emotionally marked in a positive way. This is a major part of the challenge we face.

CONSPICUOUS CONSUMPTION

We must remember that the whole thrust of marketing after the Second World War has been to promote consumerism rooted in high-carbon products and lifestyles. For over seven decades, we have been fed a constant diet that big cars, exotic holidays and wasteful consumerism are to be desired and, they tell other people who we are. This public display of status through purchased goods has been defined as 'conspicuous consumption.' The economist Thorstein Veblen first coined the term 'conspicuous consumption.' in 1899 in his classic book *The Theory of the Leisure Class*, where he used it to define 'the advertisement of one's income and wealth through lavish spending on visible items.' There are many different theoretical perspectives on conspicuous consumption, including one that derives from evolutionary biology – namely, 'costly signalling theory.' The basic premise behind this theory is that certain animals (including humans) use conspicuous display as a form of communication that signals inclusiveness fitness. However, these displays must come at a cost, in that they need to take a considerable amount of 'effort, risk, economic resources and time' to work in this respect. Take, for example, the peacock, displaying its tail to attract attention during courtship in order to signal the quality of its genetic makeup by the sheer elegance and spread of its feathers. This is obviously a 'costly signal' in that this elaborate signal makes the peacock more vulnerable to predators.

For an action to qualify as 'costly signalling,' it needs to meet the following four criteria. Firstly, it

> must be costly to the signaller in terms of economic resources, time, energy, risk or some other significant domain . . . Second,

it must be easily observable by others. Third, the display must ultimately increase the odds that the signaller will gain some fitness advantage through the display, such as increased ability to attract desirable mates. Finally, the signal must be an indicator to potential mates of some important trait or characteristic, such as access to resources, pro-social orientation, courage, health, or intelligence.

(Griskevicius et al. 2007: 86)

Expensive or luxury purchases (Veblen 1899) obviously meet these criteria (and commercial advertising, of course, is based upon this fundamental idea). The ostentatious purchase of luxury goods (the adverts tell us) will lead us to attract more friends and sexual partners through our ability to signal that we have access to the appropriate financial resources. The question is whether the purchase of more environmentally friendly or more sustainable products could potentially ever follow similar principles? Some environmentally friendly products are more expensive, so the purchasing of these products is a rather straightforward (but important) way in which inclusive fitness can be signalled (more access to financial resources). However, what happens if the environmentally friendly or low carbon products are not more expensive? Can they still signal inclusive fitness as defined by costly signalling theory? After all, they can still be configured to meet some of the criteria. For example, the selection of the environmentally friendly or low carbon products is potentially observable by others (because of the presence of labels on the products). Caring about our environment/planet could perhaps make you more desirable to others by signalling your pro-social orientation.

Griskevicius et al. (2010) suggested that there are indeed links between pro-environmental consumer choice and elevated status, and 'that activating status motives can lead people to shy away from luxury and instead choose self-sacrifice.' They argued that people are indeed willing to act pro-environmentally because it enhances their social status. They used the example of the Toyota Prius (a 'green' hybrid car that costs more than a conventional equivalent) and compared it with the Honda Civic (a cheaper but highly efficient equivalent standard car). In a survey conducted in 2007 among customers who had purchased the Toyota Prius, advertised as 'the planet's favourite hybrid,' over half of the people in the survey said that the main reason for buying the Prius was that it 'makes a statement about me.' Only a quarter of the customers bought the car because it actually had lower emissions. One owner openly admitted, 'I want people to know that I care for the environment' (Maynard 2007). In other words, the main reason for buying a Prius may be social identity and elevating social status through consumer choice.

Griskevicius et al. (2010) investigated the connection between pro-environmental behaviour and elevated status. Participants in their study were given a 'motivational prime' in the form of a short story that was aimed to prime high-status motivation. The short story required them to imagine that they were 'graduating from college, looking for a job, and deciding to go work for a large company because it offers the greatest chance of moving up.' The story went on to describe the upmarket place of work with its 'upscale lobby and nice furniture.' As the readers came to the end of the story, they 'learn that they will have an opportunity to receive a desirable promotion. The story ends as the reader ponders moving up in status relative to his or her same-sex peers' (2010: 395). In a control condition, participants were also asked to read a story of a similar length that was not designed to prime social status. Instead, the participants 'read about losing a ticket to an upcoming concert and searching through the house. After the person finds the ticket, he or she heads off to the concert with a same-sex peer' (2010: 395). There was also a second control condition where participants did not read a story, but simply had to make their product choices. After the various manipulations, participants had to imagine that they were out shopping for three different products: a car, a household cleaner and a dishwasher. For each product, there was a luxury option and an environmentally friendly option. Both options were similar in price, made by the same manufacturer and had three key features describing the product. So, for example, in the case of the dishwasher, the luxury option was described as follows: 'Sub-zero ED40 Elite Dishwasher

($1,100). Comes in choice of stainless steel or white exterior with black chrome trim. Features a revolutionary heated drying system that eliminates water spots. Has powerful water sprays but produces no sound' (2010: 404). The pro-environmental version was described as 'sub-zero Eco-trend Dishwasher ($1,100). Has a standard 40-minute running cycle. Uses a recirculating water system to save water. Is made with recycled components.' Participants saw the products on a computer screen in random order and were asked, 'If you were out shopping for a car/dishwasher/household cleaner, which of these two products would you buy?'

The study revealed that in the control condition, participants were more likely to choose the luxury options than the pro-environmental options, whereas, in the experimental group, where participants had been primed with the status motivation story, they were more likely to choose the pro-environmental option. The authors concluded, 'Activating status motives led people to increase the likelihood of choosing pro-environmental green products over more luxurious non-green products' (2010: 396).

This study tells us that pro-environmental consumer choice can relate to status and that it is possible to prime this form of behaviour. Griskevicius et al. (2010) then considered the effects of social context on this, by investigating the choice of 'luxurious non-green products' and 'green products' in a private setting (shopping online) versus a public setting (shopping in a supermarket). Participants again read the same story designed to prime status motivation, with a control group reading a story unrelated to status motivation. For the private setting condition, participants were told to 'imagine that you are shopping online by yourself at home' and in the public setting, participants were told to 'imagine that you are out shopping at a store.' Participants then had to 'indicate their preferences between three green versus three non-green products.' The items were a backpack, some batteries and a table lamp. Again, each product had a 'green' and a 'non-green' alternative that were similar in price and manufactured by the same company. The results revealed that when participants in the priming condition had to imagine that they were shopping in public, they showed an increased preference for green products compared to the control condition. However, when shopping in the private condition, participants in the priming condition actually showed a decrease in the preference for green products. The authors conclude that

> when purchases are being made in private – when reputational costs were not salient – activating status motives appears to somewhat increase the attractiveness of luxurious (non-green) products . . . status motives increased attractiveness of pro-environmental products specifically when people were shopping in public. When people were shopping in private, however, status motives increased desire for luxurious, self-indulgent non-green products.
>
> (2010: 397)

In other words, when people were aware that their choices could be observed by others and had the possibility of influencing other peoples' perception of them, they were more likely to choose pro-environmental products.

In the next study of this series, the researchers investigated what happens to behavioural choice when the green and non-green items are priced differently. They found that the experimental participants were more likely to choose green products when they were more expensive than the non-green products. However, when the non-green products were more expensive and, in addition, status motivation was activated, the green items were selected less often than their more expensive non-green counterparts. In other words, price is more effective than environmental features in signalling status.

The research by Griskevicius and his colleagues suggests that costly signalling theory may well underpin pro-environmental behavioural choice, particularly in the presence of others. In some recent research, the present authors found that participants in a shopping task were more likely to choose organic or eco brands (and luxury and well-known brands) when shopping with others than when shopping alone, which tells us something about the signalling value of organic or eco brands as well as luxury and well-known brands. They were, however, significantly more likely to choose value brands when shopping alone. But, very interestingly, low carbon footprint products didn't work in this way. The participants were significantly more likely to choose low carbon items when shopping alone than when shopping with friends (McGuire and Beattie 2016). Carbon footprint does not signal status. Our somewhat pessimistic conclusion about carbon footprint was that if we are aiming to promote low carbon products and lifestyles, then we need to rethink carbon labelling so that it is more salient to consumers (and our 'audience' as we choose the products), and we need to rethink the *values* attached to carbon footprint. We concluded that it will not be enough just to transmit the basic information about carbon footprint; rather, we need to change our underlying emotions and values about it. We need to make low carbon lifestyles fashionable (McGuire and Beattie 2016:53).

The tobacco companies made smoking fashionable through several generation of ads. These were ads about social success and popularity, about relaxation and enjoyment about the prime of life and contentment. Ads about who you are and who you could become. Perhaps we need ads about green products that do something similar, that hint at this social dimension, that tell us something about how we can position ourselves in groups through our pro-environmental behaviours. After many decades, organic and eco products are starting to possess this signalling function, so it might just be possible to do something about low carbon products and lifestyles in the future. But they need to be more visible, more blatant, not tightly packed bits of information hiding on the backs of products.

In the terminology of Kahneman, we need to appeal to System 1 and allow our immediate, automatic and emotional response to guide our consumer choices. We need more of an instant response.

7

ASSESSING OUR REAL ATTITUDE TO CLIMATE CHANGE

THE CONCEPT OF THE ATTITUDE

Over the past two decades, as we have seen, there have been many campaigns linked to climate change, often driven by high degrees of optimism shared by governments, non-governmental organisations and multinational retailers, all basing their optimism on the notion of the rational and reflective consumers – consumers who know what they want, good citizens who know their own minds. Dichter would have squirmed; Kahneman might even have squirmed a bit. The rational consumers who have expressed a degree of concern about climate change; the rational consumers who are prepared to change their ways – at least that is what they tell us (and they may even mean it). The leaders of these various campaigns have argued that it may be difficult to promote major behavioural change (it always is, they say modestly), but it's certainly possible. The first step, they say, is to 'read the mind' of the consumer (although they may not use these exact words) in order to ascertain which sections of society (or indeed all of it) are ready for change. In order to do this, they say we must access the underlying *attitudes* of the public to climate change and sustainable living. 'That's where we'll start,' they say.

The concept of the 'attitude' is the linchpin on which everything else hangs. An attitude is classically defined as 'a mental and neural state of readiness organised through experience, exerting a directive or dynamic influence upon the individual's response to all objects and situations with which it is related' (Allport 1935: 810). Leahy, the CEO of Tesco in 2007, argued, 'Customers want to do more in the fight against climate change if only we can make it easier and more affordable,' and pointed to numerous market research surveys, which seemed to support his conclusion. For example, '70% of people agree that if there is no change in the world, we will soon experience a major environmental crisis' and '78% of people say that they are prepared to change their behaviour to help limit climate change' (Downing and Ballantyne 2007). These sorts of findings are very consistent. Thus the British Social Attitudes survey (2012) revealed that 76% of people 'believe climate change is happening and that humans are, at least partly, responsible.' More recently, the Department of Energy and Climate Change (2015) in the United Kingdom found that 66% of people 'reported feeling very or fairly concerned about climate change' from a survey employing 1,981 face-to-face home interviews.

So Leahy was basing his planned initiative, which was the carbon labelling of Tesco products, on the reading of consumer minds ('they were prepared to change their behaviour,' etc.). Similarly, the UK government, in the guise of DEFRA, started from the very good assumption that 'policy action needs to be rooted in understanding and awareness of consumer behaviour' (2008: 22). They argued that we must focus on people's ability to act and people's willingness to act, and then they too engaged in mind reading. 'Many people are willing to do more to limit their environmental impact, they have a much lower level of understanding about what they can do and what would make a difference' (2008: 28). Having read the mind of the consumer, and assessed the 'mental and neural state of readiness' in Allport's words (identifying 'a positive underlying attitude to the environment' in this case), they then carried out various segmentation analyses. These analyses were used to segment the population into identifiable groups with different socio-economic profiles, consumer habits and patterns of media consumption and various campaigns were then planned – aimed at each of the segments. However, they didn't work.

So why might this be? The argument that we have been assembling in this book is that the human mind is divided into two distinct cognitive systems, each with its own properties and mode of operation, with one of these systems not open to introspection. This could be the reason why many initiatives aimed at behavioural adaptation to climate change have failed. They made the wrong basic assumption about the psychology of human beings.

THE VALUE-ACTION GAP

This hypothesis could help explain a number of things. Consider first one of the core problems in the attitude-behaviour literature. Why do people report positive attitudes about the environment, but then do very little to ameliorate the effects of their own lifestyle on the environment – the so-called value-action gap? This 'value-action' gap emerges repeatedly in the research literature in the area of consumption and elsewhere in a range of countries (McGuire and Beattie 2018). The relationship between *actual* environmental behaviour and self-reports of such behaviour is often problematic. For example, Tsakiridou et al (2008) explored the relationship between attitudes and behaviours towards organic products. They found that 50% of participants *reported* that they preferred to buy organic products, but this was contradicted by actual consumption data in that only a small proportion of those who expressed a positive attitude towards organic products actually purchased organic products. Kormos and Gifford (2014) performed a meta-analysis of the validity of self-report measures of pro-environmental behaviour and concluded that 'self-reports are only weakly associated with actual behaviour' (2014: 360). They identified some of the factors responsible for this weak relationship, including the fact that self-report measures may be 'prone to exaggeration' and that because self-report measures are

'subjective by nature; descriptors such as "*Often*," may mean different things to different participants' (2014: 360). In addition to this,
self-reports of behaviour may 'reflect individuals' perceptions of their
behaviour, behavioural intentions, or other – sometimes false – beliefs
and attitudes, rather than objective behaviour' (2014: 360). They also
say that 'limited memory or knowledge may also reduce the accuracy
of self-reports' (2014: 360).

There are clearly different ways of attempting to resolve this 'value-
action' gap. You could assume that you have a good measure of underlying attitude, but what you need to do is to add other psychological
components into the model, such as subjective norms (beliefs about
how others will behave) and perceived behavioural control (whether
you think that your behaviour will make a difference) in an attempt
to boost its predictive power (Ajzen and Fishbein 1980). Alternatively,
you can consider other economic, marketing or commercial features
of products (such as price, quality, convenience and brand familiar-
ity) that may affect consumer choice and factor those into the model
in an interactive way.

THE WRONG MEASURE OF ATTITUDE?

However, there is, of course, another possibility, which is that perhaps
we have been measuring attitudes incorrectly in the first place, or the
wrong sort of attitudes. Indeed, one might question whether our
'mental and neural state of readiness' is open to introspection, and
whether we could ever hope to report it accurately in surveys. Allport
himself seemed to show some awareness of this in his classic 1935
volume. He wrote,

> The meagreness with which attitudes are represented in con-
> sciousness resulted in a tendency to regard them as manifesta-
> tions of brain activity or of the unconscious mind. The persistence
> of attitudes which are totally unconscious was demonstrated by
> Müller and Pilzecker (1900).
>
> (Allport 1935: 801)

He clearly did not rule out the concept of the unconscious attitude, but chose to focus exclusively on the measurement of attitudes with self-report questionnaires. One of the authors has argued elsewhere (Beattie 2013) that his reasons for this particular focus were both academic and highly personal, but Allport's legacy then defined attitude measurement in psychology, and related disciplines, for many decades to come.

But interest in 'the meagreness with which attitudes are represented in consciousness'; in other words, 'implicit cognition' and 'implicit attitudes,' has been growing in the past few years, and this could lead us to think very differently about the 'value-action' gap. This research might one day tell us that the 'value-action' gap does not actually exist, because we have been measuring and factoring in the wrong measure of 'value' in the first place. Kahneman, as we have seen, argues that as human beings, we do not necessarily understand the causes and operations of our own cognitions and behaviour because of this fundamental division in our cognitive processes.

> When we think of ourselves, we identify with System 2, the conscious, reasoning self that has beliefs, makes choices, and decides what to think about and what to do. Although System 2 believes itself to be where the action is, the automatic System 1 . . . is effortlessly originating impressions and feelings that are the main sources of the explicit beliefs and deliberate choices of System 2.
>
> (2011: 21)

Greenwald (1990) has considered the accumulated effects of all of this associative activation for attitudes, our 'mental and neural state of readiness,' and argued that we may well have implicit attitudes formed on such basic processes that are not available to introspection and are indeed unconscious. The problem with this theorising about implicit attitudes was that we had no way to access implicit attitudes or measure them reliably until Greenwald developed a reaction-time-based task to measure associative connections called the Implicit Association Test or IAT (Greenwald et.al 1998). The basic premise is that when participants categorise items into two sets of paired concepts, then if the paired concepts are strongly associated, participants should be able to categorise the items faster, and with fewer errors, than if they are not strongly associated (see Figure 7.1a–d for an example of a high/low carbon footprint IAT).

In some domains, consciously reported explicit attitudes and implicit attitudes, measured through speed of association, are correlated (although the size of the correlation does vary). However, in many other domains, there seems to be little or no correlation between the two measures, and this has led Greenwald and Nosek (2008) to suggest that explicit and implicit attitudes can be 'dissociated.' When it comes to climate change, there appears to be no significant correlation between implicit and explicit measures, this time in terms of attitude to carbon footprint. Some argue that this is not that surprising and that explicit and implicit attitudes reflect the two very different information-processing systems described by Kahneman and others with different processes of acquisition. Implicit attitudes are based on

Figure 7.1a–d An example of a carbon footprint IAT (from Beattie 2010)

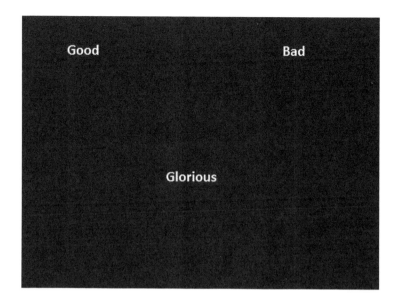

Figure 7.1b

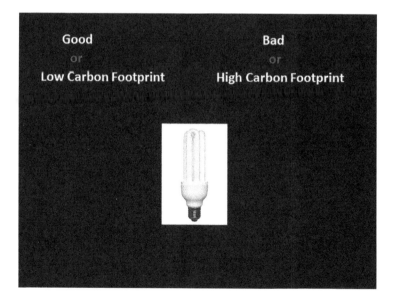

Figure 7.1c

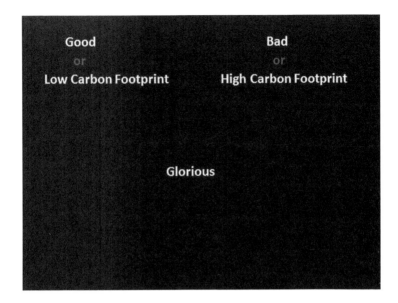

Figure 7.1d

a slow-learning associative system, whereas explicit attitudes are based on a fast learning system, which uses higher-level logic and symbolic representations. Rydell and McConnell (2006) have shown that you can change implicit and explicit attitudes with different sorts of information. Consciously accessible verbal information about a target changes the explicit attitude towards that target, whereas subliminally presented primes, 'reflecting the progressive accretion of attitude object-evaluation pairings,' changes the implicit attitude towards them. You can even change implicit and explicit attitudes in opposite directions by using associative information below the level of conscious awareness to change implicit attitudes, and consciously processed verbal material (in opposition to this) to change explicit attitudes.

So what are the possible implications of this 'divided self' – of not having one but two underlying types of attitude, for behaviour in general, and more specifically for consumer behaviour in the context of the threat of climate change? Both types of attitude can be relevant for behaviour, but under different sets of circumstances, and this is what the empirical research seems to suggest. Self-report attitudes may predict behaviour under certain situations, especially when people have the motivation and the opportunity to deliberate before making a behavioural choice (Fazio et al. 1995), but they are less good at predicting spontaneous behaviour under time pressure, or when consumers are under any sort of cognitive or emotional load. Unfortunately, time pressure, cognitive load and the absence of any opportunity to deliberate, characterises much of everyday supermarket shopping. Supermarket shopping is rarely found to be a slow, deliberate, reflective process; the shopper passes about 300 brands per minute, and each individual choice is often quick and automatic. In such contexts, unconsciously held implicit attitudes might be a better predictor of actual consumer behaviour than explicit attitudes, where an implicit attitude is defined as 'the introspectively unidentified . . . trace of past experience that mediates **R**' [where **R** is the response – the favourable or unfavourable feeling, thought, or action towards the social object]' (Greenwald and Banaji 1995: 5). In other words, habitual consumer behaviour without much opportunity or motivation to deliberate might be driven by processes not open to introspection and therefore not picked up by self-report measures. They require a different sort of measure. In the words of Greenwald and Banaji (1995: 5), 'Investigations of implicit cognition require indirect measures, which neither inform the subject of what is being assessed nor request self-report concerning it'

The concept of implicit attitude gives us a different way of thinking about the motivational basis for human action and could be a critical element in the fight against climate change. Implicit, rather than explicit attitudes, may well be underpinning everyday habitual consumer behaviours. Such behaviours may be 'sticky,' in sociological jargon, because attempts to change attitudes and behaviour just focus on certain types of messages, ignoring the associative networks of the implicit system. Recently, we have been investigating how implicit attitudes relate to how we process information relevant to climate change, assuming that the processing of relevant information is the starting point of the whole process of behavioural change. There are many persuasive messages available about climate change, but what happens if people do not see these sorts of messages? We have seen that dispositional optimism has an effect on this, but what else?

IMPLICIT ATTITUDES AND BEHAVIOUR

In one study, we attempted to determine how eye movements towards or away from iconic images of environmental damage and climate change are affected by explicit versus implicit attitudes (Beattie and McGuire 2012). We did this by projecting slides onto a computer screen, each slide containing three images, one positive image of nature, one negative image of climate change and environmental damage, and one neutral image (things like pictures of cups, plates and other everyday objects). We found that people do not focus inordinately on the negative images of environmental damage when there are other positive images and neutral images available. They usually look less than 40% of the time at the negative images. However, very importantly, those with strong positive implicit attitudes to carbon footprint were significantly more likely to focus on the negative images of environmental damage and climate change than the positive images. We also found that those with a positive implicit attitude to low carbon footprint products looked more at the negative images of climate change and environmental damage in the first 200 milliseconds compared with those with less strong positive implicit attitudes to low carbon footprint products. However, measures of explicit attitude did not predict patterns of eye movement towards the negative images in this way. It would seem that those who have strong implicit pro-low-carbon attitudes are primed to attend to these sorts of images, whereas those with strong explicit attitudes are not (they actually look less).

More recently, we considered the relationship between explicit and implicit attitudes and visual fixation of carbon labels on products (Beattie and McGuire 2015). We found that there was no significant relationship between explicit or implicit attitude to carbon footprint and the overall amount of attention devoted to the carbon label. However, there was a significant statistical association between our measure of implicit attitude and the target of the first fixation. Those individuals with the most positive implicit attitude were more likely to fixate first on the carbon footprint information (rather than 'energy' or 'price') compared with those with a more negative implicit attitude. Those with the most positive implicit attitude had a mean of 7.0 first fixations on carbon footprint, whereas those with the least positive implicit attitude had a mean of 4.5 first fixations on carbon footprint. This association did not, however, occur with explicit attitude. Those with the most positive explicit scores had a mean of 5.3 first fixations on carbon foot-print, whereas those with more negative explicit attitudes had a mean of 6.5 first fixations on carbon footprint. This difference was both in the wrong direction and non-significant. So, again, we find evidence that measures of implicit attitude, but not measures of explicit attitude, predict patterns of unconscious eye movements.

This research opens up the possibility that we may have implicit attitudes at odds with what we report (and indeed at odds with how we think about ourselves), which can nevertheless influence our everyday behaviour. But the question remains, to what extent do these implicit attitudes predict consumer choice? In a very simple study, Beattie and Sale (2011) had found that when participants were asked to select either a high carbon or low carbon goody bag at the end of an experiment measuring attitudes, those with a strong pro-low-carbon implicit attitude were more likely to select the low carbon goody bag, but only under time pressure. Very similar results had been reported by Friese et al. (2006), who also found that implicit attitude predicted the choice of a gift (a 'generic' gift versus a 'branded' gift) for taking part in the experiment, but again only under time pressure. These results are interesting, but of course, tell us very little about how people will behave in a real consumer choice situation for a number of reasons. Firstly, in terms of what might be called broad ecological considerations, consumer products are characterised by a number of different dimensions (brand, value, taste, health features, environmental implications etc.), all operating simultaneously, which could affect consumer choice at both the associative and more rational levels. Advertising is used to build brands (be they well-known brands, luxury brands, organic or eco brands or value brands) in an associative manner (Aaker and Biel 2013), and when it comes to consumer choice under time pressure, even when System 1 might be more active, these other associations might swamp any implicit associations to do with our attitudes to carbon footprint. Secondly, in terms of experimental considerations, in both Friese et al. (2006) and Beattie and Sale (2011), the choice of the reward was left until the very end of the experiment. At this point, it might have been apparent to participants that the experiment was measuring attitudes to certain attributes of products and might have produced some demand characteristics about what was or was not appropriate behaviour.

Of course, notwithstanding these points, both studies did suggest that time pressure is a critical variable in this domain and that implicit attitudes might be more predictive of behaviour when time is not freely available and when there is certainly little opportunity to deliberate. This may have particular relevance for consumer choice especially in supermarkets where much everyday shopping occurs in advanced Western nations. These kinds of considerations formed the basis for another study by the present authors (Beattie and McGuire 2016), where we analysed consumer choice of real brands as a function of both time and as a function of both implicit and explicit attitudes. In this study, we found that consumers are very sensitive to both brand information and value in their selection of products. The brands chosen most frequently under no time pressure were the well-known brands – Heinz, Kellogg's, Hovis, etc. (chosen in 38.0% of all selections, with four alternatives to choose from), followed by the value brand (32.4%). Significantly, further down the list were the organic/eco brands with 17.0% and lastly the luxury brands at 12.6%. When behavioural choice was made under time pressure, this trend became even more pronounced, and the well-known brands were selected even more frequently (pointing to the power of advertising for promoting brand recognition). Well-known brands were now chosen in 42.8% of all cases and value brands 31.4% of the time (down slightly). Organic/eco brands were now in last place with only 10.4% of selections. See Figure 7.2.

This time dimension (so characteristic of much supermarket shopping) had a statistically significant effect on consumer choice in terms of the selection of well-known brands compared to organic/eco brands. Under time pressure, consumers were significantly more likely to choose luxury brands and significantly less likely to choose organic/eco brands. Given the social and temporal aspects of much supermarket shopping, often characterised by significant time pressure, this is not an optimistic conclusion regarding environmentally sensitive choices.

We also found that those participants in our study with a positive implicit attitude to carbon footprint were guided by colour-coded carbon footprints but not by the numerical values of carbon footprint, representing the gradations of high and low carbon, within them. Given that most countries haven't introduced colour-coded carbon

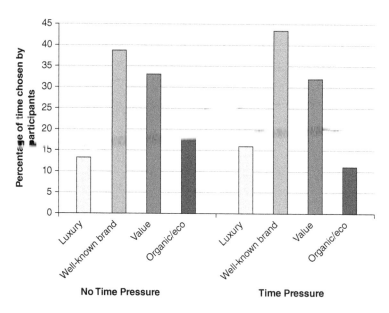

Figure 7.2 Consumer choice whilst shopping – no time pressure and time pressure (from Beattie and McGuire 2016)

footprint but have instead opted for numerical values on a plain background, this might well explain why these campaigns have, up to now, been relatively unsuccessful in promoting behavioural change and the selection of the low carbon alternatives. We also found that under time pressure, the strong pro-low-carbon implicit group did show a significant tendency in selecting low carbon items; the weak pro-low-carbon implicit group did not show a significant tendency in this regard. In other words, when participants/consumers are under time pressure (as they are in many everyday consumer situation) those with a strong implicit attitude to low carbon are more likely to shop in a sustainable way. Our measure of explicit attitude to low carbon also significantly predicted the choice of organic/eco products, but here only when the choice was not made under time pressure, suggesting that they may need more time to process the label and/or reflect on the nature of their choice.

The results of our study give us some insight into the variables that affect consumer choice and help point towards the attitudinal measures that may allow us to predict more sustainable consumer behaviour. In the case of implicit attitudes measured using the IAT, one might say that it is extraordinary that a simple reaction time measure, which simply computes the response time in a categorisation task, can predict anything at all in a separate domain. However, the simple measure predicts choice of low carbon items and even predicts the choice of organic/eco products (at least when there is more time for the consumer to reflect). The advantage of this simple measure is that participants do not seem quite so able to distort it for reasons of social desirability in order to appear greener than they really are compared to self-report measures. It may, therefore, provide us with a simple diagnostic tool to test the public's actual readiness to go green in the fight against climate change, and this could turn out to be very important indeed. One could imagine redoing the segmentation analyses of DEFRA and other leading organisations where one attempted to profile the population in terms of both explicit and implicit attitudes rather than relying merely on what people say. See Figure 7.3.

EXPLICIT ATTITUDE

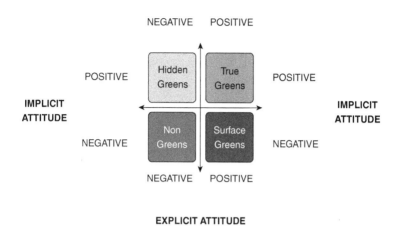

Figure 7.3 Example of implicit attitude/explicit attitude segmentation analysis

Of course, the research also raises some very general issues about whether consumers are dissociated in a number of respects and whether two separate (but potentially interacting) systems of unconscious/implicit and conscious/explicit attitudes really do exist. It would seem that in some domains, this notion of implicit attitudes, deriving from various associative connections and operating unconsciously alongside our more reflective attitudes (and indeed conflicting with them on occasion), might have some credibility (Beattie 2013). Such a view, after all, might not surprise those psychologists who worked in the 1930s alongside some of the major tobacco companies to promote smoking (subliminally) through the association of smoking with societal success, social acceptance, masculinity or femininity and confidence. It might not even have surprised Gordon Allport in his early work on racism and 'the inner conflict' (Allport 1954). It is certainly an idea worth exploring further in the domain of consumption and climate change. If we really do have a 'divided self' when it comes to our underlying attitudes towards the environment, then this could be critical in the battle against climate change. After all, many of us say that we know that we need to adapt our behaviour as consumers in the light of the threat of climate change, but then actually do nothing. Until we start to promote low carbon products and low carbon lifestyles in a way that impinges on our automatic, unconscious system, little may actually change in this regard. We cannot leave choice of low carbon products solely to reason and reflection; it could be far too late. As Kahneman (2011) himself has noted, System 2 (the system of reason and reflection) can be very lazy indeed; it leaves a great deal to System 1, and System 1 is currently prioritising well-known brands and value brands over those with the right environmental properties. System 1, in the domain of consumption, is directing us to choose those things that we have been taught to value – big brands (and status) and economical brands (and money) rather than environmental brands. This may well need to change. By all means, let us continue to write (and read) the editorials in the quality newspapers about climate change and what we must all do. But at the same time, let us think about how to promote low carbon lifestyles as something to do with a new sort of societal status, fun, sexy, necessary, caring, cooperative, clever, perceptive, confident, a must have, the next big thing, a new revolution, in a way that System 1 might notice, and let's make sure that its more public to allow us to signal our green behaviours. Moreover, if we have to borrow from the years of (chilling) success of the tobacco industry in promoting smoking and learn from the way they used associative networks, then so be it. At least, we will then know that it was good for something. They knew that there were two levels of processing, one conscious, one unconscious; we are slowly waking up to this idea.

CONCLUDING REMARKS

Climate change is the most pressing problem that we face, or have ever faced. Science tells us (unambiguously) how severe this problem is and what effect it is going to have on our planet. And yet the response of the public and some politicians has been extraordinarily sanguine. Concern about climate change seems to have gone down in recent years, rather than up, as the scientific evidence has grown stronger. This change in direction of concern seems to have occurred around the time of the Kyoto Protocol, and the economic threat to the energy companies and other big business, and the subsequent emergence of a vigorous 'debate' on the topic, which mirrors a very similar earlier debate about the possibly harmful effects of smoking (which, with the passage of time, just looks plainly ridiculous). The public are becoming more polarised about climate change in terms of their beliefs and attitudes, and many do not see it as a threat that will actually affect them – perhaps future generations or countries overseas, but not them personally. Many campaigns have been tried without any real success to change this. There also seems to be a very severe disconnect between the reported attitudes of those who do believe in climate change and want to do something, and their subsequent actions.

We have tried to address many of these issues in this short book. We have considered cognitive and social biases, and how people maintain that warm glow of optimism in the light of compelling scientific evidence that spells out the devastating effects of climate change. We have discussed the false consensus effect where we all seem to believe that we are the majority and that it is people who do not share our views who are odd and distinctive in some way. We have reviewed the evidence that emotion and automatic responses guide what we see and what we remember and how we subsequently frame the problem. We have considered one fundamental problem with human beings, which is that they don't really have a mind after all. They have two distinct sets of cognitive processes, and the difficulty with much of the psychological work underpinning climate change campaigns, and carbon labelling and all that great advice about reducing carbon footprint, is that this basic fact has not been recognised. The problem with many aspects of everyday consumer behaviour is that they are very fast and automatic, and it is these automatic responses that we need to work on and change through climate change campaigns. We need to rethink how to market green lifestyles to affect these fast, automatic processes and to offer and promote the positive aspects of changing behaviour to make it more environmentally friendly. There has been too much focus on the negatives and too much emphasis on guilt and fear, without offering a positive rewarding alternative. We looked at the tobacco industry to see how they targeted the unconscious mind in the days when psychology as a discipline had dismissed this approach as being too unscientific. Gordon Allport, the founder of social psychology, had always assumed that explorations of unconscious motivations would take psychology down a blind alley (after Freud's clumsy attempts to psychoanalyse him). It was a psychoanalyst in the end, Ernest Dichter, who exploited the power of unconscious motivations to sell cigarettes, and he did this with spectacular and ruthless efficiency. At the same time, he recognised that we also have a rational mind, and he fed that rational mind with enough misinformation ('there's a confounding variable in the relationship between smoking and lung cancer – guilt, stress, personality, take your pick') to allow them to enjoy the smoking habit by alleviating some of their own personal guilt. Recently, psychology has returned to a recognition of dual processes in the mind, bolstered enormously by the work of the Nobel Laureate Daniel Kahneman, and this may hold some clues as to how we may proceed in the future.

We can all present the rational case for climate change. The IPCC have been doing this for years. But that is simply not enough. And when you remind those who direct climate change campaigns of this, they merely hit the audience with huge dollops of fear or guilt, as if these are the only alternatives. Instead, we need to think in a different way about how to promote pro-environmental behaviours with subtle and sophisticated messages about how joint pro-environmental action links us together (just like smoking), helps us connect (like smoking), helps us to derive greater status (like smoking), makes us more successful (like smoking), offers us all a long and healthy future (unlike smoking).

A few years ago, we heard Paul Polman, the CEO of Unilever, remark at a conference, 'There is no profit in a dead planet.' It was as plain and as straightforward as that, and that, as they say in business, is the bottom line. We need to be more ruthless in getting people to recognise the threat using sophisticated social marketing techniques, borrowing ideas from wherever we need to, including the tobacco companies (and you can just imagine their reaction!).

Donald Trump might just then, and only then, get the message.

FURTHER READING

BOOKS

Beattie, G. (2018). *The Conflicted Mind: And Why Psychology Has Failed to Deal With It*. London: Routledge.

Hoffman, A. J. (2015). *How Culture Shapes the Climate Change Debate*. Stanford: Stanford University Press.

Kahneman, D. (2011). *Thinking, Fast and Slow*. London: Penguin.

Marshall, G. (2015). *Don't Even Think About It: Why Our Brains Are Wired to Ignore Climate Change*. London: Bloomsbury Publishing

Oreskes, N. & Conway, E. M. (2010). *Merchants of Doubt*. London: Bloomsbury.

FILMS

An Inconvenient Truth (2006)

An Inconvenient Sequel: Truth to Power (2017)

Merchants of Doubt (2014)

REFERENCES

Aaker, D. A. & Biel, A. L. (2013). *Brand Equity & Advertising: Advertising's Role in Building Strong Brands*. London: Psychology Press.

Ajzen, I. & Fishbein, M. (1980). *Understanding Attitudes and Predicting Social Behaviour*. London: Prentice Hall.

Allport, G. W. (1954). *The Nature of Prejudice*. Oxford, England: Addison-Wesley.

Allport, G. W. Attitudes. In C. Murchinson (Ed.), *A Handbook of Social Psychology*. Worcester, Massachusetts: Clark University Press.

Barthes, R. (1957). *Mythologies* (A. Lavers, trans.). New York: Hill.

Beattie, G. (2010). *Why Aren't We Saving the Planet? A Psychologist's Perspective*. London: Routledge,

Beattie, G. (2011). Making an action film. Do films such as Al Gore's *An Inconvenient Truth* really make any difference to how we think and feel about climate change? *Nature Climate Change*, 1, 372–374.

Beattie, G. (2012). Psychological effectiveness of carbon labelling. *Nature Climate Change*, 2, 214–217.

Beattie, G. (2013). *Our Racist Heart? An Exploration of Unconscious Prejudice in Everyday Life*. London: Routledge.

Beattie, G. (2016). How Donald Trump bullies with his body language. *The Conversation*. http://theconversation.com/how-donald-trump-bullies-with-his-body-language-664681 Accessed 16th March 2018.

Beattie, G. (2017). The psychology behind Trump's awkward handshake . . . and how to beat him at his own game. *The Conversation*. http://theconversation.

com/the-psychology-behind-trumps-awkward-handshake-and-how-to-beat-him-at-his-own-game-73143 Accessed 22nd May 2018.

Beattie, G. (2018). *The Conflicted Mind: And Why Psychology Has Failed to Deal With It*. London: Routledge.

Beattie, G., Marselle, M., McGuire, L. & Litchfield, D. (2017). Staying over-optimistic about the future: Uncovering attentional biases to climate change messages. *Semiotica*, 218, 21–64.

Beattie, G. & McGuire, L. (2011). Are we too optimistic to bother saving the planet? The relationship between optimism, eye gaze and negative images of climate change. *International Journal of Environmental, Cultural, Economic and Social Sustainability*, 7, 241–256.

Beattie, G. & McGuire, L. (2012). See no evil? Only implicit attitudes predict unconscious eye movements towards images of climate change. Semiotica, 192, 315–339.

Beattie, G. & McGuire, L. (2015). Harnessing the unconscious mind of the consumer: How implicit attitudes predict pre-conscious visual attention to carbon footprint information on products. *Semiotica*, 204, 253–290.

Beattie, G. & McGuire, L. (2016). Consumption and climate change: Why we say one thing but do another in the face of our greatest threat. *Semiotica*, 213, 493–538.

Beattie, G., McGuire, L. & Sale, L. (2010). Do we actually look at the carbon footprint of a product in the initial few seconds? An experimental analysis of unconscious eye movements. *The International Journal of Environmental, Cultural, Economic and Social Sustainability*, 6, 47–66.

Beattie, G. & Sale, L. (2011). Shopping to save the planet? Implicit rather than explicit attitudes predict low carbon footprint consumer choice. *The International Journal of Environmental, Cultural, Economic and Social Sustainability*, 7, 211–232.

Beattie, G., Sale, L. & McGuire, L. (2011). An inconvenient truth? Can extracts of film really affect our psychological mood and our motivation to act against climate change? *Semiotica*, 187, 105–126.

Bechara, A., Damasio, H., Tranel, D. & Damasio, A. R. (1997). Deciding advantageously before knowing the advantageous strategy. *Science*, 275, 1293–1295.

British Social Attitudes Survey. (2012). British social attitudes. www.bsa.natcen.ac.uk/latest-report/british-social-attitudes-29/transport/belief-in-climate-change.aspx Accessed 1st January 2018.

Brown, R. & Kulik, J. (1977). Flashbulb memories. *Cognition*, 5, 73–99.

Crane, F. G. & Crane, E. C. (2007). Dispositional optimism and entrepreneurial success. *The Psychologist-Manager Journal*, 10, 13–25.

Department of Energy and Climate Change. (2015). DECC public attitudes tracking survey. www.gov.uk/government/collections/public-attitudes-tracking-survey Accessed 14th March 2018.

Department for Environment Food and Rural Affairs. (2008). A framework for pro-environmental behaviours. www.gov.uk/government/uploads/system/uploads/attachment_data/file/69277/pb13574-behaviours-report-080110.pdf Accessed 29th January 2018.

Department of Health. (2014). Stop the rot: New campaign highlights how cigarettes 'rot' the body from the inside. www.gov.uk/government/news/stop-the-rot-new-campaign-highlights-how-cigarettes-rot-the-body-from-the-inside Accessed 19th March 2018.

Dichter, E. (1960). *The Strategy of Desire*. London: Transaction.

Downing, P. & Ballantyne, J. (2007). Tipping point or turning point. *Social Marketing and Climate Change*. London: Ipsos-MORI. www.ipsos-mori.com.

Ehrenreich, B. (2009). *Bright-Sided: How the Relentless Promotion of Positive Thinking Has Undermined America*. New York: Holt.

Ehrenreich, B. (2010). *Smile or Die: How Positive Thinking Fooled America and the World*. London: Granta.

Eysenck, H. J. (1966). *Smoking, Health and Personality*. London: Four Square

Fazio, R. H., Jackson, J. R., Dunton, B. C. & Williams, C. J. (1995). Variability in automatic activation as an unobtrusive measure of racial attitudes. A bona fide pipeline? *Journal of Personality and Social Psychology*, 69, 1013–1027.

Fredrickson, B. L. & Branigan, C. (2005). Positive emotions broaden the scope of attention and thought-action repertoires. *Cognition & Emotion*, 19, 313–332.

Friese, M., Wänke, M. & Plessner, H. (2006). Implicit consumer preferences and their influence on product choice. *Psychology & Marketing*, 23, 727–740.

Gifford, R. (2011). The dragons of inaction: Psychological barriers that limit climate change mitigation. *American Psychologist*, 66, 290–302.

Gifford, R., et al. (2009). Temporal pessimism and spatial optimism in environmental assessments: An 18-nation survey. *Journal of Environmental Psychology*, 29, 1–12.

Global Risk Report. (2016). 11th edition. www3.weforum.org/docs/Media/ TheGlobalRisksReport2016.pdf Accessed 10th January 2018.

Greenwald, A. G. (1990). What cognitive representations underlie attitudes? *Bulletin of the Psychonomic Society, 28*, 254–260.

Greenwald, A. G. & Banaji, M. R. (1995). Implicit social cognition: Attitudes, self-esteem, and stereotypes. *Psychological Review, 102*, 4–27.

Greenwald, A. G., McGhee, D. E. & Schwartz, J. L. (1998). Measuring individual differences in implicit cognition: The implicit association test. *Journal of Personality and Social Psychology, 74*, 1464–1480.

Greenwald, A. G. & Nosek, B. A. (2008). Attitudinal dissociation: What does it mean? In R. E. Petty, R. H. Fazio & P. Brinol (Eds.), *Attitudes: Insights From the New Implicit Measures* (pp. 65–82). Hillsdale, NJ: Erlbaum.

Griskevicius, V., Tybur, J. M., Sundie, J. M., Cialdini, R. B., Miller, G. F. & Kenrick, D. T. (2007). Blatant benevolence and conspicuous consumption: When romantic motives elicit strategic costly signals. *Journal of Personality and Social Psychology, 93*, 85–102.

Griskevicius, V., Tybur, J. M. & Van den Bergh, B. (2010). Going green to be seen: Status, reputation, and conspicuous conservation. *Journal of Personality and Social Psychology, 98*, 392–404.

The Guardian. (2004). Tsunami highlights climate change risk, says scientist. www.theguardian.com/education/2004/dec/31/highereducation.uk1 Accessed 22nd March 2018.

Hoffman, A. J. (2015). *How Culture Shapes the Climate Change Debate*. Stanford: Stanford University Press.

The Independent. (1996). Eysenck took £800,000 tobacco funds. www.inde pendent.co.uk/news/eysenck-took-pounds-800000-tobacco-funds-1361007.html Accessed 27th February 2018.

Intergovernmental Panel on Climate Change (1995) *Second Assessment Report — Climate Change* (J.T. Houghton, L.G. Meira Filho, B.A. Callander, N. Harris, A. Kattenberg & K. Maskell, Eds.). Cambridge: Cambridge University Press.

Intergovernmental Panel on Climate Change. (2007). *Climate Change 2007: The Physical Science Basis* (S. Solomon, D. Qin, M. Manning, Z. Chen, M. Marquis, K. B. Averyt, N. Tignor & H. L. Miller, Eds.). Cambridge: Cambridge University Press.

Intergovernmental Panel on Climate Change. (2013). *Climate Change 2013: The Physical Science Basis. Contribution of Working Group I to the Fifth Assessment Report of the Intergovernmental Panel on Climate Change* (T. F. Stocker, D. Qin, G. K. Plattner,

M.B. Tignor, S. K. Allen, J. Boschung, A. Nauels, Y. Xia V. Bex, & P. M. Midgley Eds.). Cambridge: Cambridge University Press.

Intergovernmental Panel on Climate Change (2014). *Climate Change 2014: Mitigation of Climate Change. Working Group III Contribution to the Fifth Assessment Report of the Intergovernmental Panel on Climate Change* (O. Edenhofer, R. Pichs-Madruga, Y. Sokona, J. C. Minx, E. Farahani, S. Kadner, K. Seyboth, A. Adler, I. Baum, S. Brunner, P. Eickemeir, B. Kriemamm, J. Savolainen, S, Schlömer, C. von Stechow, & T. Zwickel). Cambridge: Cambridge University Press.

Intergovernmental Panel on Climate Change. (2015). *Climate Change 2014: Synthesis Report. Contribution of Working Groups I, II and III to the Fifth Assessment Report of the Intergovernmental Panel on Climate Change* (The Core Writing Team, R. K Pachauri & L. Maeyer, Eds.). Cambridge: Cambridge University Press.

Isaacowitz, D. M. (2006). Motivated gaze: The view from the gazer. *Current Directions in Psychological Science, 15*, 68–72.

Kahneman, D. (2011). *Thinking, Fast and Slow.* London: Penguin.

Kasinger, C. (2018). The mind meld of Bill Gates and Steven Pinker. *The New York Times.* www.nytimes.com/2018/01/27/business/mind-meld-bill-gates-steven-pinker.html Accessed 16th March 2018.

Kormos, C. & Gifford, R. (2014). The validity of self-report measures of proenvironmental behavior: A meta-analytic review. *Journal of Environmental Psychology, 40*, 359–371.

Leviston, Z. & Walker, I. (2012). Beliefs and denials about climate change: An Australian perspective. *Ecopsychology, 4*, 277–285.

Luo, J. & Isaacowitz, D. M. 2007. How optimists face skin cancer information: Risk assessment, attention, memory, and behavior. *Psychology and Health, 22*, 963–984.

Marshall, G. (2015). *Don't Even Think About It: Why Our Brains Are Wired to Ignore Climate Change.* London: Bloomsbury Publishing.

Mathews, A. & MacLeod, C. (2002). Induced processing biases have causal effects on anxiety. *Cognition & Emotion, 16*, 331–354.

Maynard, M. (2007). Say 'Hybrid' and Many People Will Hear 'Prius'. The New York Times http://www.nytimes.com/2007/07/04/business/04hybrid.html?_r=0. (Accessed 24th January 2018).

McCright, A. M. & Dunlap, R. E. (2011). The politicization of climate change and polarization in the American public's views of global warming, 2001–2010. *The Sociological Quarterly, 52*, 155–194.

McGuire, L. & Beattie, G. (2016). Consumers and climate change: Can the presence of others promote more sustainable consumer choice? *The International Journal of Environmental Sustainability*, 12, 33–56.

McGuire, L. & Beattie, G. (2018). Talking green and acting green are two different things: An experimental investigation of the relationship between implicit and explicit attitudes and low carbon consumer choice. *Semiotica*.

Mosing, M. A., Zietsch, B. P., Shekar, S. N., Wright, M. J. & Martin, N. G. (2009). Genetic and environmental influences on optimism and its relationship to mental and self-rated health: A study of aging twins. *Behavioral Genetics*, 39, 597–604.

Müller, G. E. & Pilzecker, A. (1900). Expedmentelle beitrage zur lehre vom gedachtni. *Zeitschrift Psychologie*, 1, 1–300.

National Endowment for Science, Technology and the Arts. (2008). Selling sustainability. *Seven Lessons from Advertising and Marketing to Sell Low-Carbon Living.* www.nesta.org.uk/sites/default/files/selling_sustainability.pdf Accessed 19th March 2018.

Oreskes, N. & Conway, E. M. (2010). *Merchants of Doubt.* London: Bloomsbury.

Pahl, S., Harris, P., Todd, H. A. & Rutter, D. R. (2005). Comparative optimism for environmental risks. *Journal of Environmental Psychology*, 25, 1–11.

Pettigrew, M. P. & Lee, K. (2011). The 'father of stress' meets 'big tobacco': Hans Selye and the tobacco industry. *The American Journal of Public Health*, 101, 411–418.

Pierre-Louis, K. (2017). It's cold outside: Cue the Trump global warming tweet. *New York Times*, 28th December 2017. www.nytimes.com/2017/12/28/climate/trump-tweet-global-warming.html Accessed 16th March 2018.

Rayner, K., Pollatsek, A., Ashby, J. & Clifton, C. (2012). *Psychology of Reading.* London: Psychology Press.

Ross, L. (1977). The intuitive psychologist and his shortcomings: Distortions in the attribution process. In L. Berkowitz (Ed.), *Advances in Experimental Social Psychology* (pp.173–220). New York: Academic Press.

Rydell, R. J. & McConnell, A. R. (2006). Understanding implicit and explicit attitude change: A systems of reasoning analysis. *Journal of Personality and Social Psychology*, 91, 995–1008.

Scheier, M. F., Matthews, K. A., Owens, J. F., Magovern, G. J., Lefebvre, C., Abbott, A. & Carver, C. S. (1989). Dispositional optimism and recovery from coronary artery bypass surgery: The beneficial effects on physical and psychological well-being. *Journal of Personality and Social Psychology*, 57, 1024–1040.

Schulz, R., Bookwala, J., Knapp, J. E., Scheier, M. & Williamson, G. M. (1996). Pessimism, age and cancer mortality. *Psychology and Aging*, 11, 304–309.

Segerstrom, S. C., Taylor, S. E., Kemeny, M. E. & Fahey, J. L. (1998). Optimism is associated with mood, coping, and immune change in response to stress. *Journal of Personality and Social Psychology*, 74, 1646–1655.

Seligman, M. E. (2002). *Authentic Happiness: Using the New Positive Psychology to Realize Your Potential for Lasting Fulfillment*. New York: Free Press.

Selye, H. (1976). *The Stress of Life*. New York: McGraw-Hill.

Sharot, T. (2011). The optimism bias. *Current Biology*, 21, 941–945.

Slovic, P., Finucane, M., Peters, E. & MacGregor, D. G. (2002). Rational actors or rational fools: Implications of the affect heuristic for behavioral economics. *The Journal of Socio-Economics*, 31, 329–342.

Stern, N. H. (2006). *Stern Review: The Economics of Climate Change*. London: HM treasury.

Taylor, S. (1998). The MacArthur research network on socioeconomic status and health. www.macses.ucsf.edu/research/psychosocial/optimism Accessed 2nd March 2018.

Tsakiridou, E., Boutsouki, C., Zotos, Y. & Mattas, K. (2008). Attitudes and behaviour towards organic products: An exploratory study. *International Journal of Retail & Distribution Management*, 36, 158–175.

Tukker, A., Huppes, G., Guinée, J., Heijungs, R., de Koning, A., van Oers, L., Suh, S., Geerken, T., Van Holderbeke, M., Jansen, B. & Nielsen, P. (2005). *Environmental Impact of Products (EIPRO): Analysis of the Life Cycle Environmental Impacts Related to the Total Final Consumption of the EU25*. Brussels: IPTS/ESTO, European Commission Joint Research Centre.

Tversky, A. & Kahneman, D. (1973). Availability: A heuristic for judging frequency and probability. *Cognitive Psychology*, 5, 207–232.

UK Climate Change Risk Assessment 2017 Synthesis Report: Priorities for the Next Five Years. (2016). www.theccc.org.uk/tackling-climate-change/preparing-for-climate-change/climate-change-risk-assessment-2017/ Accessed 1st August 2016.

Unilever. (2013). Unilever sustainable living plan. www.unilever.com.tw/Images/slp_Unilever-Sustainable-Living-Plan-2013_tcm13-388693_tcm206-395956.pdf Accessed 1st January 2018.

USGCRP (2017). *Climate Science Special Report: Fourth National Climate Assessment*, Volume I (D.J. Wuebbles, D.W. Fahey, K.A. Hibbard, D.J. Dokken, B.C. Stewart & T.K. Maycock, Eds.]. U.S. Global Change Research Program, Washington, DC, USA, 470 pp., doi: 10.7930/J0J964J6.

Veblen, T. (1899). *The Theory of the Leisure Class*. New York: The New American Library.

Wang, S., Corner, A., Chapman, D., & Markowitz, E. (2018). Public engagement with climate imagery in a changing digital landscape. *Wiley Interdisciplinary Reviews: Climate Change*, 9, e509.

Witte, K. & Allen, M. (2000). A meta-analysis of fear appeals: Implications for effective public health campaigns. *Health Education & Behavior*, 27, 591–615.

World Health Organization. (2017). Climate change and human health. www.who.int/globalchange/en/ Accessed 15th March 2018.

World Resource Institute. (2014). www.wri.org/blog/2014/05/history-carbon-dioxide-emissions Accessed 10th January 2018.

Yang, J. Z. & Kahlor, L. A. (2012). What, me worry? The role of affect in information seeking and avoidance. *Science Communication*, 35, 189–212.

Zajonc, R. B. (1980). Feeling and thinking: Preferences need no inferences. *American psychologist*, 35, 151–175.